THE NATIONAL HISTORIC PRESERVATION ACT

United States Congress House of Representatives Committee on Resources, Subcommittee on National Parks

The BiblioGov Project is an effort to expand awareness of the public documents and records of the U.S. Government via print publications. In broadening the public understanding of government and its work, an enlightened democracy can grow and prosper. Ranging from historic Congressional Bills to the most recent Budget of the United States Government, the BiblioGov Project spans a wealth of government information. These works are now made available through an environmentally friendly, print-on-demand basis, using only what is necessary to meet the required demands of an interested public. We invite you to learn of the records of the U.S. Government, heightening the knowledge and debate that can lead from such publications.

Included are the following Collections:

Budget of The United States Government	Code of Federal Regulations
Presidential Documents	Congressional Documents
United States Code	Economic Indicators
Education Reports from ERIC	Federal Register
GAO Reports	Government Manuals
History of Bills	House Journal
House Rules and Manual	Privacy act Issuances
Public and Private Laws	Statutes at Large

THE NATIONAL HISTORIC PRESERVATION ACT

OVERSIGHT HEARING

BEFORE THE

SUBCOMMITTEE ON NATIONAL PARKS

OF THE

COMMITTEE ON RESOURCES
U.S. HOUSE OF REPRESENTATIVES

ONE HUNDRED NINTH CONGRESS

FIRST SESSION

Thursday, April 21, 2005

Serial No. 109-7

Printed for the use of the Committee on Resources

Available via the World Wide Web: http://www.access.gpo.gov/congress/house
or
Committee address: http://resourcescommittee.house.gov

U.S. GOVERNMENT PRINTING OFFICE

20-807 PS   WASHINGTON : 2005

For sale by the Superintendent of Documents, U.S. Government Printing Office
Internet: bookstore.gpo.gov   Phone: toll free (866) 512–1800; DC area (202) 512–1800
Fax: (202) 512–2250   Mail: Stop SSOP, Washington, DC 20402–0001

C O N T E N T S

OVERSIGHT HEARING ON THE NATIONAL HISTORIC PRESERVATION ACT

Thursday, April 21, 2005
U.S. House of Representatives
Subcommittee on National Parks
Committee on Resources
Washington, D.C.

The Subcommittee met, pursuant to notice, at 10:00 a.m, in Room 1324 Longworth House Office Building, Hon. Devin Nunes [Chairman of the Subcommittee] presiding.

Present: Representatives Nunes, Christensen, Kildee, Duncan, Radanovich, and Fortuno.

STATEMENT OF THE HON. DEVIN NUNES, A REPRESENTATIVE IN CONGRESS FROM THE STATE OF CALIFORNIA

Mr. NUNES. The Subcommittee will come to order. Good morning. Today the Subcommittee on National Parks will conduct an important oversight hearing on the National Historic Preservation Act.

As part of their testimony, I have asked the witnesses to share their thoughts with the members of the Subcommittee on a discussion draft prepared by the Subcommittee to amend the Act.

As my colleagues are aware, the Subcommittee last conducted a hearing on the Act in 2003. Since that time, the Subcommittee has taken a much closer look into the development of the procedures associated with the Act, which has resulted in the discussion draft.

I look forward to hearing the thoughts of my colleagues and the witnesses.

I want to welcome all of you here today and thank you all for being here and your attendance. And now I recognize Mrs. Christensen for her opening statement.

[The prepared statement of Mr. Nunes follows:]

Statement of The Honorable Devin Nunes, Chairman, Subcommittee on National Parks

The Subcommittee will come to order.

Good morning. Today, the Subcommittee on National Parks will conduct an important oversight hearing on the National Historic Preservation Act. As part of their testimony, I have asked the witnesses to share their thoughts with the Members of the Subcommittee on a Discussion Draft prepared by the Subcommittee to amend the Act.

As my colleagues are aware, the Subcommittee last conducted a hearing on the Act in 2003. Since that time, the Subcommittee has taken a much closer look into the development of the procedures associated with the Act, which has resulted in

(1)

the Discussion Draft. I look forward to hearing the thoughts of my colleagues and the witnesses.

————

STATEMENT OF THE HON. DONNA M. CHRISTENSEN, A DELEGATE FROM THE VIRGIN ISLANDS

Mrs. CHRISTENSEN. Thank you, Mr. Chairman.

Mr. Chairman, I join you this morning in welcoming our witnesses here today and thank them for assisting the Subcommittee in gathering information regarding the changes that you are proposing to the National Historic Preservation Act.

As you know, Mr. Chairman, the National Historic Preservation Act is the bedrock upon which all Federal historic preservation programs are built.

The Act created the Advisory Council, which Mr. Nau chairs, as well as the National Register of Historic Places and Historic Preservation Fund. The Act also ensures that the Federal Government avoids inadvertently damaging historic resources.

The results speak for themselves, Mr. Chairman: 1.2 million structures, objects, districts, and sites identified, evaluated, and protected because they were significant in the life of this country and the lives of the American people.

More than 60 of those listed properties are in Fresno and Tulare Counties in California, Mr. Chairman, while more than 80 are in my district of the U.S. Virgin Islands.

This 40-year legacy of effective historic preservation requires that the sweeping changes you are proposing to the Act be reviewed with great care. The very real concern that such changes may undermine the effectiveness of the Act, and thus threaten this legacy, requires the Subcommittee to set a very high bar regarding these proposals.

Mr. Chairman, we are going to hear testimony today that your proposal to narrow the scope of Section 106 to include only those historic properties that are already documented could have devastating impact. For example, many sites that are culturally significant in Native Americans would not meet this test because we have been so slow to recognize the significance of these resources.

Conversely, relatively new areas, which have yet to be listed or found eligible, such as the World Trade Center site, could fail this test as well. This is despite the fact that few could doubt the site's historic significance.

In that regard, Mr. Chairman, I ask unanimous consent to enter into the record a letter from the Coalition of 9/11 Families explaining their opposition to the discussion draft.

Mr. NUNES. Without objection.

[The letter from the Coalition of 9/11 Families follows:]

APRIL 18, 2005

VIA FACSIMILE (202) 225-3404 FAX

Hon. Devin Nunes
Chairman
Subcommittee on National Parks, Recreation and Public Lands
1017 Longworth HOB
Washington, DC 20515

Dear Congressman Nunes:

The Coalition of 9/11 Families represents more than 4,000 individuals who lost family members on September 11, 2001. I am writing to you on behalf of the Coalition to express our concerns about proposed amendments to the National Historic Preservation Act (NHPA), which will soon be considered by the House Subcommittee on National Parks, Recreation and Public Lands. For more than a year the Coalition has served as a Consulting Party in the NHPA Section 106 review of several federally funded undertakings at the World Trade Center site. I can assure you that had it not been for the requirement that "eligible" properties be included in evaluating the effects of those projects on historic resources, the remains of the Twin Towers, most especially the physical remains that delineate the twin tower footprints at bedrock would have continued to be ignored and would have been completely destroyed.

For more than a year, the Coalition, together with other Consulting Parties such as the National Trust for Historic Preservation and the Historic Districts Council has been fighting—with only partial success—to have the historic significance of the physical remains of the World Trade Center recognized. If the property owner, the Port Authority of New York and New Jersey, had the right to refuse to have the World Trade Center site declared eligible for the National Register—as the proposed amendments would allow—there would have been no consideration of how construction of their proposed new commercial/transportation projects would effectively destroy the location where our loved ones were murdered. Nearly half of the victims have not been identified, nor will they be at this time due to technological limitations and the site continues to be the only place where families can go to pay respects to their loved ones.

The existing Section 106 process is far from perfect, but it has afforded the Coalition an opportunity to be heard and have input into the design of Port Authority's proposed facility. The original World Trade Center was not listed on the National Register. None of the federal agencies involved, nor the Advisory Council on Historic Preservation, would accede to our request that a formal determination of eligibility be made by the Secretary of the Interior. Requests from Members of Congress went unheeded. It was only the requirement that "eligible" properties be identified that caused the redevelopers of the World Trade Center site to consider our concerns. If only properties listed on the National Register had been considered during the Section 106 process, not only the Coalition, but every citizen who believes that September 11 was a transcendently significant event in our nation's history would have suffered irreparable harm.

REGARDS,

ANTHONY GARDNER, BROTHER OF HARVEY JOSEPH GARDNER III,
EXECUTIVE BOARD MEMBER, COALITION OF 9/11 FAMILIES

cc: Congressman Shays
    Congresswoman Maloney
    Congressman Pombo
    Subcommittee Members

Mrs. CHRISTENSEN. Mr. Chairman, we simply cannot risk these types of unintended consequences without evidence of widespread, well-documented, and ongoing problems which cannot be dealt with under the Act as written.

Isolated, anecdotal assertions, nor industry complaints which can be addressed administratively justify such fundamental and potentially harmful alterations to this statute.

We look forward to the thoughts of our witnesses on these matters, Mr. Chairman, and thank you.

Mr. NUNES. Thank you, Mrs. Christensen. At this point, I would like to ask the witnesses to stand and please your right hand and repeat after me.

[Witnesses sworn.]

Mr. NUNES. Thank you. With that, I do want to say that we will be having votes this morning, and so what we would like to do is try to limit the testimony to 5 minutes so we can—because we do have your testimony for the record. That way, we can get through the testimony and then get into questions.

So with that—I don't know. Mr. Kildee, do you have an opening statement?

Mr. KILDEE. Can I make just about a 1-minute opening statement.

Mr. NUNES. Sure. Yes. The Gentleman is recognized.

Mr. KILDEE. I appreciate that. Thank you very much.

STATEMENT OF THE HON. DALE E. KILDEE, A REPRESENTATIVE IN CONGRESS FROM THE STATE OF MICHIGAN

Mr. KILDEE. Mr. Chairman, I have strong concerns about Section 4 of the discussion draft for proposed amendments to the National Historic Preservation Act. I received letters from several tribes, the National Congress of American Indians, the United South and Eastern Tribes, and other organizations raising concerns that Section 4 would eliminate a provision in current law that protects as sacred sites and cultural items of Indian tribes.

Section 4 would also undermine the Federal regulations designed to implement the current law. The regulatory process requires, among other things, tribal consultation and establishes a process for determining whether a site is eligible for inclusion in the National Register.

The Federal requirements in the National Historic Preservation Act and other laws and Executive Orders were established to fulfill promises we made to Native Americans that their cultural and historical sites, places of worship, and burial grounds would be protected and preserved.

Last September, President Bush signed an Executive Memorandum in honor of the opening of the National Museum of the American Indian that reiterates the adherence to the principles set forth in a previous Executive Order relating to tribal consultation and coordination.

Section 4 violates the spirit of the several Federal laws and mandates that provide for the protection of cultural and historical sites of our country's first Americans.

I want to thank the Chairman for not introducing this draft prior to today's hearing so that we may have an opportunity to work cooperatively with all interested parties in developing alternative solutions. And I look forward to hearing from the witnesses today, and I thank you very much for your indulgence.

[The prepared statement of Mr. Kildee follows:]

Statement of The Honorable Dale E. Kildee, a Representative in Congress from the State of Michigan

Mr. Chairman, I have strong concerns about Section 4 of the discussion draft of proposed amendments to the National Historic Preservation Act.

I have received letters from several tribes, the National Congress of American Indians, the United South and Eastern Tribes and other organizations raising concerns that Section 4 would eliminate a provision in current law that protects the sacred sites and cultural items of Indian tribes.

Section 4 would also undermine the Federal regulations designed to implement the current law.

The regulatory process requires, among other things, tribal consultation and establishes a process for determining whether a site is eligible for inclusion in the National Register.

The Federal requirements in the National Historic Preservation Act and other laws and Executive Orders were established to fulfill promises we made to Native Americans that their cultural and historical sites, places of worship, and burial grounds would be protected and preserved.

Last September, President Bush signed an Executive Memorandum in honor of the opening of the National Museum of the American Indian that reiterates the adherence to the principles set forth in a previous Executive Order relating to tribal consultation and coordination.

Section 4 violates the spirit of several Federal laws and mandates that provide for the protection of cultural and historical sites of our country's first Americans.

I want to thank the Chairman for not introducing this draft prior to today's hearing so that we may have an opportunity to work cooperatively with all interested parties on developing alternative solutions.

I look forward to hearing from the witnesses today.

Thank you.

Mr. NUNES. Thank you, Mr. Kildee.

With that, we will recognize Mr. Peter Blackman for five minutes.

STATEMENT OF PETER F. BLACKMAN, PROPERTY OWNER, LOUISA, VIRGINIA

Mr. BLACKMAN. Chairman Nunes, members of the Subcommittee, thank you for inviting me to speak before you.

My name is Peter Blackman. I own a farm that is a contributing property to the National Register listed Green Springs Historic District in Central Virginia, 12 miles east of Charlottesville.

I am currently engaged in litigation with the National Park Service over plans to renovate my house, a piece of which you see in that photograph.

The nub of the lawsuit brought by the United States is the purported conservation easement it holds on the property as part and parcel to the National Register Program.

The issue I wish to address today is Section 2(a) of the discussion draft concerning Section 101(a)(6) of the Historic Preservation Act. This section currently allows the Secretary to find a property eligible for the National Register over the objections of a property owner.

The effect of this provision is to run roughshod over the property rights of that owner through a back door eligibility designation, which can have the same restrictions as a normal listing. The proposed amendment, by closing this loophole, is long overdue. I applaud this, a step in the right direction that returns an important property right protection to homeowners.

I respectfully submit to the Subcommittee, however, that this amendment does not go far enough. A property owner needs more than a veto power over a potential National Register listing. He should be able to opt out or withdraw from the National Register at any time. The National Register is supposed to be elective, an honor. Supposedly, you can do anything you wish with your house without penalty—even demolish your house within the limits of state and local law.

That is what the Park Service literature trumpets time and again, and what you are told when being wooed to list your property on the National Register.

Alas, that is only part of the story. The National Park Service and others will use the National Register as a bludgeon against the property owner to trample his property rights, if they can. To them, your property, once listed, is just a resource. To them it is not a home.

This danger may sound far off and academic. I am here today to tell you that it is happening now. It is happening to me, and I am not alone.

The cause of this problem is what I call the "add-ons" to the National Register. These add-ons are most often local or state preservation regulation that kicks in when a property has National Register status of some kind. In my case, the add on was an alleged easement, which the Park Service assumed from a private non-profit organization in 1978, then placed with the Shenandoah National Park to manage. Every step of this process, by the way, was carried out without any apparent statutory authority to do so, in contravention of basic administrative law and due process.

The Park Service has used the easement it claims to have on my property to apply as mandatory requirements what is known as the Secretary of Interior's standards for rehabilitation to their review of renovation plans of my house. It has applied these guidelines in a punitive manner. These standards were never intended to be used this way. Like the National Register itself, these standards were meant to be non-compulsory and to be treated flexibly, as at most a starting point in discussions with a property owner.

But to give you an idea of what the Park Service has done, the have prevented me from remediating extensive toxic mold and fixing dire structural problems, invoking these standards on a house that can only be seen from the road, three quarters of a mile away.

A Federal judge agreed that these standards are not supported by the easement document the government relied upon. They have done all this in the name of preservation. As to their objections to my larger plans, it can be summed up as his: my modifications or additions, which the government attorney herself described as, I quote "gorgeous," are one of two things. Most often there are too much in the style of the original house. Other times, they are different from the original house, and thereby objectionable. Go figure.

Now, I can tell you that I am not the only person, even in my community, who has encountered this morass of vague, shifting standards, but most property owners end up having no choice but to give in. The government has a huge advantage in terms of time and money when a dispute arises.

The Park Service knows this. They know that they can mess with a property owner. It does not cost them personal time or money. Yet, their decisions can disrupt a property owner's life and home as they have mine. I would mention before my time is up a few other issues my situation raises. One is that the National

Register was meant to protect a property owner from Federal action. That is the purpose of Section 106 of the Historic Preservation Act. That is the section that triggers an intricate review whenever a Federal action might negatively impact a National Register property. But the Park Service has inverted the notion of Federal undertaking, a term defined in the regulations under the Act, to use it as a weapon against me without any support under that definition. They have actually asserted that their aesthetic review of my house constitutes a Federal undertaking. It makes no sense.

In my case also, there has been an improper delegation to a local non-profit organization. This has been done without the Park Service vetting the group. In fact, the Park Service itself has repeatedly expressed reservations about this group's I quote "closely held agenda."

I could also speak about the Park Service's abuse of the whole FOIA, or Freedom of Information Act, process and their retaliatory behavior.

And the last point, the documents I will offer the Committee should speak for themselves.

Before I close, I would like to offer to the Subcommittee documents pertaining to my litigation. I have here the entire court record, including a transcript from an evidentiary hearing, appellate briefs on a narrower certified question about the easement's validity under the common law, a question argued just yesterday before the Virginia Supreme Court, in which the government attorney admitted that she had no cases to support her proposition, and also documents surrounding a failed attempt by the government to hold me in criminal contempt for an alleged violation of an injunction. The charge was thrown out because the government tried to bypass going to the Federal judge hearing the case in a blatant violation of the Federal Rules of Criminal Procedure.

The court record also includes many illustrative documents as attachments, including, of course, the disputed easement. In addition, I offer a fuller written statement about the district I live in and my dealings with the National Park Service leading up to the litigation, and I also have copies of the correspondence relating to an investigation initiated by my Congressman, Eric Cantor, and two FOIA, Freedom of Information, requests I made in 2003.

Finally, I also have letters from neighbors with similar concerns and letter from the Property Rights Foundation of America speaking of similar problems that have occurred in other geographic areas.

Once again, I thank the Subcommittee for affording me the opportunity to address my concerns. Thank you.

[The prepared statement of Mr. Blackman follows:]

Statement of Peter F. Blackman, Property Owner, Louisa, Virginia

My name is Peter Blackman. I own a farm that is a contributing property to National Register listed Green Springs Historic District in Central Virginia, twelve miles east of Charlottesville. I am currently engaged in litigation with the National Park Service over plans to renovate my house. The nub of the lawsuit, brought by the United States, is a purported conservation easement it holds on the property as part and parcel to the National Register program. On advice of counsel, I am limited in how I can comment on the litigation itself, but I offer to the Subcommittee the full court record to date, among other documents.

The issue I wish to address today is Section 2(a) of the discussion draft regarding proposed amendments to the Historic Preservation Act. Specifically, I am concerned with Section 101(a)(6) of the Act. This Section currently allows the Secretary to find a property eligible for the National Register over the objections of a property owner. The effect of this provision is to basically run roughshod over the property rights of that owner through a back door eligibility designation, which can have the same restrictions as a normal listing. The proposed amendment, by closing this loophole, is long overdue. I applaud this, a step in the right direction that returns an important property right protection to homeowners.

I respectfully submit to the subcommittee, though, that this amendment does not go far enough. A property owner needs more than a true veto power over a potential National Register listing. He should be able to opt out or withdraw from National Register at any time. The National Register is supposed to be elective, after all, and an honor. You can do anything you wish with your house without penalty, even demolish your house, within the limits of state and local law. That is what the Park Service literature trumpets time and again and what you are told when being wooed to list your property on the National Register.

Alas, that is only part of the story. The National Park Service and others will use the National Register as a bludgeon against the property owner and trample his property rights, if they can. To them, your property, once listed, is just a "resource;" to them, it is not a home.

This danger may sound far-off and academic. I am here today to tell you that it is happening today. It is happening to me, and I am not alone!

The cause of this problem is what I would call the "add-ons" to the National Register. These add-ons are most often local or state preservation regulation that kicks in when a property has National Register status. Here in Washington, to use just one example, if a property is listed on the National Register, you cannot demolish any part of it without the approval of a mayor's agent, something that is seldom given. It does not matter that the property was not on the local list of landmarks. The National Register is enough to trigger this rule.

In my case, the add-on was an alleged easement, which the Park Service assumed from a private nonprofit organization in 1978, then placed with the Shenandoah National Park to manage. Every step of this process, by the way, was carried out, I believe, without any apparent statutory authority to do so, in contravention of basic administrative law.

The Park Service has used the easement it claims to have on my property to apply as mandatory requirements what is known as the Secretary of Interior's Standards for Rehabilitation to their review of renovation plans for my house. It has applied these guidelines in a punitive manner. These standards were never intended to be used this way. Like the National Register's itself, these standards were meant to be non-compulsory and to be treated flexibly, as at most a starting point in discussions with a property owner. But to give you an idea what the Park Service has done, they have prevented me from remediating extensive toxic mold and fixing dire structural problems, invoking these standards. A federal judge agreed that these standards are not supported by the easement document the government relied upon. They have done all this in the name of "preservation." I have some pictures to show you what I mean. SHOW PHOTOS And they were on record even disallowing me to do more limited work, which would have no effect on the long-term cosmetic appearance of the house, all in the name of "preservation." I submit, with their form of preservation, their valuable "resource," my home, may collapse!

As to their objections to my larger plans, it can be summed up as this: my modifications or additions, which the government attorney herself described as "gorgeous," are one of two things: most often, they are too much in the style of the original house! Other times, they are different from the original house, and thereby objectionable! Go figure!

Now I can tell you that I am not the only person, even in my community, who has encountered this morass of vague, shifting standards, but most property owners end up having no choice but to give in. The government has a huge advantage in terms of time and money when a dispute arises. The Park Service knows this. They know that they can then mess with a property owner. It does not cost them personal time or money! Yet their decisions can disrupt a property owner's life and home, as they have, mine.

I wish I could go into greater detail. I would like to mention, before my time is up, or if the subcommittee will permit me, that there are a few other issues that my situation raises that bear its looking into.

One is that the National Register was meant to protect a property owner from federal action. That is the purpose of Section 106 of the Historic Preservation Act. That is a section that triggers an intricate review whenever a federal action, such as a highway, might negatively impact a National Register property. But the Park Service has inverted the notion of "federal undertaking," a term defined in the regulations under the Act, to use it as weapon against me, without any support under that definition. They have actually asserted that their aesthetic review of my house constitutes a federal undertaking. It makes no sense. I have no doubt they have done this with others.

In my case, also, there has been an improper delegation to a local nonprofit organization. This has been done without the Park Service vetting the group. In fact, the Park Service itself has repeatedly expressed reservations about this group's "closely held agenda."

I could also speak about the Park Service abuse of the whole FOIA process, and but for the litigation, the possible retaliatory behavior of the Park Service. I think, though, the documents I provide may speak for themselves on this last point.

Before I close, I will quickly summarize the documents I am leaving with you that help support what I have alluded to in this speech. The court record includes a transcript from an evidentiary hearing, appellate briefs on a narrower certified question about the easement's validity under the common law, a question argued just yesterday before the Virginia Supreme Court, and documents surrounding a failed attempt by the government to hold me in criminal contempt for an alleged violation of an injunction. The charge was thrown out because the government tried to bypass going to the federal judge hearing the case. The court record includes many illustrative documents as attachments, including, of course, the disputed easement. In addition, I offer a fuller written statement about the district I live in and my dealings with the National Park Service leading up to the litigation. I also have attached to that are correspondence relating to an investigation initiated by Congressman Eric Cantor and two Freedom of Information requests I made in 2003, and some documents uncovered in the FOIA investigations.

Once again, I thank the subcommittee for affording this opportunity to address my concerns.

————

SUPPLEMENTAL STATEMENT TO TESTIMONY

I currently own and reside in the Historic Green Springs District located in Louisa County, Virginia, approximately 12 miles to the east of Charlottesville. I have lived there since July 1, 2002. My property, 275 acres known as Eastern View Farm, is considered a contributing property to a district-wide listing to the National Register, which is administered by the National Park Service. It is not separately listed. This is an important distinction. The simple farm house has, even in its decrepitude, considerable charm—that is why I bought it—but it is of a design and type common to Central Virginia and has no historical or architectural significance. On the application by the District to the National Register, under section 8 which is supposed to detail what is significant about the house, it is entirely silent about my house, whereas other houses in the district are described there in considerable detail. All that the National Register application contains about my house is a brief, somewhat inaccurate description under section 7. It is my understanding that the standard practice of the National Register, when it evaluates proposed renovations and changes to a house, is to rely solely on section 8. In my case, the Park Service treated every item of the description given in section 7 as it were in section 8.

None of this would matter to me except the Park Service also held a purported conservation easement on my property. The purported easement was used by the Park Service to apply otherwise non-compulsory standards provided in the Secretary of Interior's Standards for Rehabilitation as if binding, and to do so in a punitive manner, despite the fact that no tax credits or deductions were ever received by an owner of Eastern View, either at the time of the grant of the alleged easement, or thereafter. In applying the Standards in a compulsory manner to me, the Park Service has maintained, in effect, that they possess the sole authority for interpreting these standards. Further, the Park Service has made no provision for an appeal. They have consistently maintained throughout my dealings with them that they are willing to continue discussions and entertain revised plans, but there is nothing specific holding them to a timetable or to adhere to any set of procedures. It is because these standards were meant to be elective that they are written loosely. A property owner could simply opt out if he disagreed. [1] The easement document itself did not

---

[1] W. Brown Morton, currently a professor at Mary Washington College in Virginia and a drafter of the Secretary's Standards, has recently stated on numerous occasions that the Standards

Continued

support the use of these Standards. It could not have, as the alleged easement was executed in 1973, a number of years before there were any Secretary's Standards in existence. The purported easement provided several vague standards of its own, which might be summarized as changes and additions to the house must be in the style of the existing structure. This standard is at loggerheads with the overriding approach of the Secretary's Standards, which prescribe that anything new be done in a manner that is distinguishable from the existing structure, so that a passerby might not be confused about the historic evolution of the house. Whereas the easement document explicitly allows additions, the Secretary's Standards discourage them.

The house, at the time I bought it, was in wreck condition. I bought the house with the idea of renovating it. I had successfully renovated a "pre-war" New York City apartment, circa 1928, also in wreck condition, a few years before, and I looked forward to tackling the same sort of project in a rural setting. I could not imagine that anyone would be against the kind of sensitive renovation I would do. I would add that the house itself sits centered on the property's 275 acres and is a half-mile from the nearest road frontage, which is wooded. Only from short stretches of the road, approximately three quarters of a mile from the house, can it be glimpsed. Trees around the house obstruct much of that view during the summer months. There is nothing in the easement document itself, by the way, which precludes me from planting trees to block the view entirely.

Several substantial changes were made to the house from the time of the listing on the National Register of the District. None of the changes were made with the approval of the Park Service, nor did the Park Service ever object to these changes, which my FOIA request showed they had knowledge of None of the changes to the house were ones that in any way enhanced the house's architectural historic integrity, such as it was. The house when I bought it was at best marginally habitable. While I did move in and rough it, many people would have regarded it as unlivable. Among the problems I encountered in 2002, and this is not an exhaustive list, were a front porch falling off the house, another porch whose roof was structurally unsound; rotting siding, long past its useful life; inadequate insulation; many damaged structural members, with such things as the base sill upon which the house rests being badly water and termite damaged; and water damage on the interior walls throughout the house from rain seeping through rotten, broken windows. One could see light from outside coming through the exterior walls, and vines growing through them. To give you an idea, in the first winter, my propane heat bill was well in excess of $1,000 per month for a house that was 3,500 square feet. The bill was at least four times what most would have considered a normal amount, and for that, there were rooms that on cold days were completely unusable. The house did not retain heat. Water pipes, even those housed in interior walls, would freeze. I might have well been living in a tent!

In September 2003, the eye of Hurricane Isabel passed over my house. I and two others worked nonstop from 3 P.M. until 11 P.M. sopping up water penetrating the walls and ceiling. When the storm passed, it left behind additional water damage and serious toxic mold throughout the house. Patches of thick black mold were growing on the interior walls of four rooms.

Before I go into the tortuous relationship I had with the Park Service starting shortly after I bought the property, a little background on the Green Springs Historic District is in order. In the early 1970s, a proposed state prison facility disturbed some of the local homeowners, and they struck upon the idea of using rural conservation as a means to defeat it. They created a nonprofit, Historic Green Springs, Inc. ("HGSI"), to hold a number of conservation or preservation easements, which a federal court actually found were dissimilar from one another, noting that they "failed to prohibit in all cases subdivision and development of the land." [2] Moreover, the easements were rife with ambiguities and poor draftsmanship. Each of these property owners was then a member of this organization. Shortly thereafter, there was a takeover of the organization by a few members who then expelled anyone who opposed their agenda.

HGSI soon after its creation applied to be listed on the National Register as a historic district. At the time the Park Service designated the district on the National Register, the Department of Interior ("DOI") accepted an assignment of the easements from HGSI. DOI placed the administration of these easements with the Shenandoah National Park, which itself is about 80 miles from the district. The federal government owns no land in or by the District. The purported easement document

were meant to be a flexible tool and at most a starting point for negotiation with the property owner.
[2] Historic Green Springs, Inc. v Bergland, 497 F.Supp. 839, 843 (1980).

itself states "nothing herein shall be construed to convey a right to the public of access or use of the properties."

The way the Park Service conducted its inquiry into the District during the 1970s sparked litigation—the District has been an engine for litigation ever since. In 1980, there was a key decision, Historic Green Springs, Inc. v. Bergland, in which the designation of the District on the National Register was ruled invalid. Congress, by fiat, shortly afterwards restored the designation.

The alleged easement covering my property has architectural and subdivision restrictions. It is the architectural restrictions that precipitated a dispute between the NPS and me. Currently, my easement is the subject of litigation in the federal district court and the Supreme Court of Virginia. The Supreme Court heard arguments on April 20 as to whether the restrictions are cognizable and therefore even valid under the Virginia common law. I have attached a copy of the full court record to date, including the briefs prepared for the Supreme Court.

Even if the easement is found to be cognizable under Virginia law, there are serious issues whether the Park Service has the statutory authority to hold it. The Historic Sites Act of 1935 is the basis for the Park Service to hold any easement, but that act, in section 1, declares its purpose as being to "preserve for public use historic sites" and "building," and the alleged easement actually explicitly states there is no public access to the property. No where in Title 16 is the Secretary of Interior, who accepted the assignment of the easements, given the authority to place such easements in the Shenandoah National Park. Further, none of the Shenandoah National Park sections of Title 16 allow it to hold such easements, which are manifestly not adjoining the park. Even if the park has the right, it committed a number of serious violations of administrative law. One of the most egregious was involving HGSI in the review process on my property. After HGSI assigned most of the alleged easements it held in 1978, it continued to have a tight relationship which the Park Service. From 1980 through 1991, the Park Service and HGSI actually had a memorandum of understanding by which HGSI had a role in monitoring the supposed easements. The memorandum was not renewed thereafter because of complaints from many property owners and what the Park Service itself called HGSI's "closely-held agenda." By the time I moved into the community, however, the Park Service was turning to HGSI for virtually every decision relating to the area. Yet as a Freedom of Information Act investigation of mine revealed, the Park Service never did anything to audit and review HGSI, its legitimacy, et. al. The Park Service actually admitted that they had no procedures to monitor such a "partnership." Never did the Park Service offer any justification for its ties with HGSI. HGSI is clearly not a community group, in the sense of an organization representing all the affected property owners. I was never invited into the organization, and as I indicated above, many property owners were expelled some years ago. A glance at its charter discloses that its membership need not even live in the area. Nonetheless, the Park Service has called HGSI its "Partner" on many occasions.

Once I moved into my house, I started to plan how to renovate it. The Park Service came to visit my property unannounced several times, all in violation of the easement. The president of HGSI, Ms. Ely, told me what I could and could not do without my house, all before I had formulated plans, and I would add, her opinion was unsolicited. I became disturbed by the role of Ms. Ely, as I saw no justification for her participation, a lack of accountability by her or her organization, a lack of legitimate expertise in architecture or architectural history, among other reasons. Alas, my concerns were unavailing with the Park Service. I complained to my Congressman, Eric Cantor, who initiated the first of several investigations. The Park Service response in all the investigations was to evade or deny all the charges, despite my having provided considerable documentary evidence of my concerns. However, the Park Service made an implied promise after the first investigation that they would no longer involve HGSI and Ms. Ely in the review process of my home. In my first FOIA search of Park Service documents I discovered that in fact they not only went right on involving Ms. Ely, but they were even communicating every step of the response they were formulating to Congressman Cantor's inquiry, a document in which they had implied they would not be consulting her.

After I hired an architect in Fall, 2002, he drew up plans which were submitted to the Park Service in February, 2003. Those plans, and several revisions afterwards, were rejected on the basis of the Secretary's Standards. Sometimes the reason was that the change or addition was too similar in style to the existing house. Sometimes the reason was the opposite: it was not enough alike. The Park Service could seem to be expressing approval for an element of the plan, but they never gave a go ahead on anything. Throughout their correspondence they spoke of a willingness to continue a dialogue, but they offered, and had, no official appeal process, as is a basic administrative law protection to a citizen in a governmental discretionary review. Their own literature directed at local architectural review boards says that providing for an appeal is an essential part of a legitimate program. Especially frustrating for me in this review was how they would base their pronouncements on erroneous or speculative beliefs about my house. An example was how they rejected plans for me to enlarge basement windows in the front of the house. The existing windows were small transom windows. The Park Service insisted that these were original to the house. Anyone versed in architectural history would have known that in fact the current basement was probably once a ground floor with more graceful windows. But even if you did not have this base of knowledge, a quick glance from the outside showed the outline of the former windows, which had been covered with concrete!

The Park Service did make one adjustment after I complained about HGSI; they told my architect that they routinely involve the Virginia Department of Historic Resources. In my FOIA search, I found no evidence that the Park Service had ever done this before, except in regard to the processing of tax credits. The Park Service treated this involvement as a review under Section 106 of the Historic Preservation Act, notwithstanding that Section 106 clearly did not apply. The purpose of this section was to protect property owners from deleterious effects of federal action. The section applies when there is a federal undertaking. This requires either an expenditure of federal funds or the issuance of a license. Neither were pertinent to the aesthetic review of my house. A classic federal undertaking is the building of an interstate highway. If such a road were to affect a National Register property, then Section 106 would call for a review on how such an undertaking would impact the "resource," or the historic buildings covered on the National Register. The idea was to deter heedless negative developments, whatever they might be, involving the federal government, without a full weighing of the potential consequences. That highway might still be built, as planned, but only after there was a full analysis of its impact on a historic property. Basically, the scheme was to ensure that one arm of the federal government wouldn't be working at cross-purposes with another, that historic preservation was a worthy objective and should not be forgotten. To regard the review of my plans as a Section 106 undertaking was to invert the law's purpose and instead of protecting the property owner against a federal intrusion, to treat the property owner as the intrusion.

Even if the delegation to the Virginia Department had legitimacy, and their obstinate use of the Secretary's Standards justified, the Park Service tainted the objectivity of such review by basically telling the Virginia Department the conclusions it wished to have validated. (This is revealed in the correspondence between the Park Service and the Virginia Department.) It is my understanding that the Virginia Department receives funding from the Park Service, a relationship that might undermine its independence.

By early fall, the Virginia Department was apparently on the verge of approving of my plans. Suddenly, the Park Service changed their tune, minimizing the role of the Virginia Department, consulting with other parts of the Park Service to get the negative opinion they were seeking, and invoking a new standard, NPS 28, which is intended for Park Service owned or managed properties, and so clearly irrelevant to my home, which was neither. This NPS 28, needless to say, had no basis in the alleged easement document, was different from the Secretary's Standards, and until then, had never been mentioned, in a notorious flouting of administrative law.

I mention that I made a FOIA requests. In these requests the NPS improperly withheld information and possibly documents too. For example, they declined to provide documents on the basis of attorney client privilege, refusing to disclose even the names of the parties so involved. Even if the document were privileged, the Freedom of Information Act clearly requires that such names are not protected information.

Finally, it is my belief that the Park Service has acted against me on numerous occasions with a retaliatory motive—retaliation for my letters to my Congressman, retaliation for questioning how they conduct their business. I believe a close reading of their correspondence and emails strongly suggest this. In addition, someone I know, without my permission, actually called a senior person at the Park Service about my case. This individual supposedly ranted on about how they were going to get Blackman.

———

[The letter submitted for the record by The Property Rights Foundation of America follows:

THE PROPERTY RIGHTS FOUNDATION OF AMERICA, INC.
P.O. BOX 75, STONY CREEK, NEW YORK 12878 — 518/696-5741
WEBSITE: WWW.PRFAMERICA.ORG
E-MAIL: PRFA@PRFAMERICA.ORG

APRIL 19, 2005

The Honorable Devin Nunes
Chairman, National Parks Subcommittee
United States House of Representatives
1333 Longworth House Office Building
Washington, DC 20515

Re: National Historic Districts Subcommittee Hearing - April 21, 2005

Dear Chairman Nunes:

National Historic Districts are an important concern to private property owners. The Property Rights Foundation of America receives many requests for help to deal with strictures on private property and requirements for expensive studies related to historic and archeological preservation. However, for fear of retribution from the government officials with whom they have to deal, these property owners are afraid to "go public" with their stories. As a result, and most regrettably, I cannot refer a single property owner complaining of these egregious examples of bureaucratic intrusion on private property rights to testify before your subcommittee.

A large proportion of the historic and archeological preservation issues that come to our organization deal with New York State, where the state agency that handles designations of National Historic Districts is the New York State Office of Parks, Recreation and Historic Preservation, which I'll refer to as NYS Parks. One point that stands out is the dishonesty of NYS Parks by misleading the public about the enforcement potential as a result of a designation of a site or historic district, whether state of federal. Typical of the false disclaimers by NYS Parks is that on their web site (downloaded copy enclosed):

"There are no restrictions placed on private owners of registered properties. Private property owners may sell, alter or dispose of their property as they wish, although an owner who demolishes a certified registered property may not deduct the costs of demolition from his/her federal income tax."

During the designation process, NYS Parks has been successful in quieting public concerns about the impact of historic registration on private property owners. Afterwards, when a proposed specific project is up for government review, the enforcement takes place behind the scenes, when NYS Parks steps in, and where the local permitting process, the New York State Department of Environmental Conservation permitting process, and the like must comply with the State Environmental Quality Review Act (SEQRA). Typical of various states' "mini-NEPAs," SEQRA requires that any "state action" (lower case) consider the impact of the permit on significant historic and archeological sites, notably, those on the state or National Register. State "action" under this law is not restricted to the construction of state, federal, or local government projects such as highways, prisons, and the like, but includes state actions that are simply decision-making processes-most commonly, the permit process. Consideration of the impact of the project on a designated historic site can be very expensive, involving the hiring of experts for extensive professional studies of the proposal and contrived "alternatives." The permit may only be issued after this expense is augmented by "mitigations," such as expensive changes to the project plan to make it have what the NYS Parks considers to be less "impact" on a registered site.

The Glimmerglass Heritage National Register Historic District

The Glimmerglass Heritage National Register Historic District in Otsego County, New York, illustrates the deception on the part of advocates involved in the designation process and the forceful participation of NYS Parks in the local permit process once the registered district is in place.

Because several property owners from the area of the proposed 15,000-acre Glimmerglass district contacted the Property Rights Foundation of America when the designation was being debated during the spring of 1989, and because PRFA was contacted afterwards by a severely impacted property owner, I'm able to use the example of the Glimmerglass district to relate the problems inherent in the overall designation process and how it pans out. However, my remarks will not reveal the identity of the property owner who sought help from PRFA.

Early that year, a lively debate was taking place around Cooperstown, New York, where the Glimmerglass district was being proposed for an area around Otsego Lake. On March 26, 1999, the Cooperstown newspaper, The Freeman's Journal (copy enclosed), reported, "Officials with the New York State Historic Preservation Office hope to schedule a meeting in May at the Otsego County Courthouse to address public concerns about the proposed Glimmerglass Heritage National Register District."

"We want to use the courthouse because it seems we'll need a large space. We've had a lot of comments," said Kathleen LaFrank, the SHPO's historic preservation program analyst, according to the Journal.

"LaFrank said she is surprised by the number of people opposing the district," reported the Journal. The newspaper noted her remark that "some people seem not to believe that being in a district on the National Register of Historic Places will not compromise their property rights."

At the request of several people in the Glimmerglass area, I sent a letter to the editor of The Freeman's Journal, which was published on May 7 (copy attached). I explained how inclusion in the National Historic Register results in regulation of private property because of SEQRA being applied during the local building permit process. "SEQRA," I pointed out, "is one of the most powerful and often used environmental laws in this state."

In addition, I pointed out that the problems for the property owner do not necessarily stop with difficulties dealing with government authorities. "The owner may also be denied a mortgage if a bank judges that the use of the property will be restricted as a result of the historic registration."

I asked, "Why did the officials representing the State of New York deceive the public by not revealing SEQRA's enforcement link to designation to the National Register?"

The Journal published a reply by Robert J. Poulson, Jr., Project Chairman, Cooperstown, a few days later (copy attached). He pronounced that my letter was entirely wrong and was "alarmist." He alleged that the designation protects property rights. He said that designation would protect property owners from the actions of federal or state agencies, using a highway widening as an example, because they would have go through "not only the SEQRA process, but a special historic preservation review that will at least require the agency to mitigate the negative impact on your property."

The Cooperstown Crier later reported on meetings that NYS Parks held about the proposed district. Their article quoted Bob Kuhn, Historic Preservation Program Director of the NYS Parks, focusing on the millions of dollars in grants and tax breaks that designation makes available.

"Designation does not place local requirements on you. It does not mean that because of designation that some higher level of review is required," said Kuhn, according to the Crier. "You can paint your house lime green, you can add a modern addition, you can burn it to the ground. The state and federal government can't stop you."

The state review panel approved the Glimmerglass Heritage National Register Historic District on June 18, 1999, later to be followed by the NYS Parks commissioner's approval and referral to the National Park Service. On the occasion of the approval, The Daily Star on June 22 reported that Robert Kuhn, the NYS Park's historic coordinator, had explained at a hearing in February that "(H)is department only reviews publicly funded projects and will not be overseeing how homeowners and others take care of private property." (copy attached)

After the Glimmerglass designation was in place, NYS Parks was never held accountable for its deception. At the same time, it used the heavy weight of its office to enforce the designation.

On November 21, 2003, I received an e-mail from a private property owner within the Glimmerglass district.

"Well, it finally happened. The Glimmerglass designation is even MORE than SHPO said it would be!" the property owner declared.

He wrote that he had spent in excess of $100,000 on engineering and architectural development plans to construct his buildings on commercial property on the north end of Otsego Lake, replacing ones that were so dilapidated that the county codes officer said that they were condemnable.

"After 9 months of pushing and pulling the town through SEQRA, and getting them ready to issue a negative declaration, lo and behold, SHPO says my plans are not in keeping with the character of the district. They were ready to issue a letter of resolution indicating adverse impact before we even had a chance to present our side."

In later correspondence, he declared, "they out right lied to us!"

"I remember getting the information and saying to my wife that this could be trouble," he continued. "Then I read the articles and felt assured that this designation would only be the cause of positive results. No one, me included, understood that SHPO basically controls the permitting of state agencies. But then again, why would ordinary folks have cause to understand this. The issue was brought up by a few of the better informed, but those concerns were "allayed" by Ms. LaFrank and Mr. Kuhn. I have found in the newspaper archives several quotes that say just so! And now when we refer back to these quotes I am told that I am taking them out of context. Interestingly, the NYSPARKS website blatantly lies as well, saying once again that historical designation will not place any controls on the private property owner: "you can alter, dispose (etc)." Well...it seems that no we can't!"

The story of deception during the Glimmerglass Heritage National Register Historic District illustrates the need for reform.

Spin-off Effects of Regulatory Impact of National Historic Sites

This hearing represents a greatly needed public forum about the regulatory impact of listing in the National Historic Register. Another area of potential impact is on the availability of mortgage listing. The inflexibility inherent in designation has been known to dampen the interest of lenders.

In September 1996, I stayed at the Rochell Haus, a gracious old farmhouse with a view of Seneca Lake, in Hector, New York, that had been converted to a bed and breakfast. Susan Rochell, who with her husband Henry owned the Rochell Haus, told me of their travail obtaining a mortgage to do alterations to the interior and rear of the house to convert it for their new business. The banks declined to give them a mortgage for their alterations to make the circa 1830s house into a bed and breakfast on the grounds that the building was on the National Historic Register. Finally, they approached their Congressman for help. The only solution, which was then in his hands, Mrs. Rochell told me, was to have the house deleted from the National Historic Register. The Congressman used his influence to have the historic registration for the house finally removed, and the bank gave the mortgage to the Rochells.

Recommendations:

No property should be included within a National Historic District or Site or for listing for eligibility for registration within a District or as a Site without the written consent of the property owner.

Every property owner within a proposed National Historic District or Site or listing for eligibility as such, or within a State Historic District being developed with the intent of inclusion in the National Register, should be clearly notified of the enforcement consequences under both state and federal law of the listing on the register or placement on the eligible list.

Pressure to Increase the Number of National Historic Sites

A troubling new development related to the National Trust for Historic Preservation could spell pressure to increase the number of listings, whether justified or not, and have impact on private property rights. According to Eric Gibson, in an article entitled "Trust Us: This is How Travel Gets "Historic'," on April 15 in The Wall Street Journal (copy attached). The National Trust for Historic Preservation is reacting to potential Congressional cutback in their funding by replacing the congressional appropriation with full reliance on private funding. The organization intends to "expand the number and diversity of historic places associated with the Trust." Hotels will be an important source of new historic sites, with sites such as Boston's Omni Parker House where JFK proposed to Jackie mentioned as an example.

Gibson fears trivializing the historic designation, but, for property owners, a more practical concern could arise. Historic districts might proliferate, with many property owners caught inside who would opt out if allowed. Or historic sites might be chosen at the behest of localities or neighbors who could benefit from the listing, but the property owner would not be allowed to decline to be listed.

The potential commercialization of National Historic Sites argues for increased protections for property owners. Honest information on regulatory impact and mandated property owner consent for National Historic Register listing and eligibility listing are crucial.

Additional Recommendation:

The Congress should deliberate about the possible conflict with the Congressional Charter of the National Trust for Historic Preservation if listing on the National Historic Register is commercialized.

Thank you for convening the National Parks Subcommittee hearing about issues related to listing on the National Historic Register.

RESPECTFULLY,
CAROL W. LaGRASSE, PRESIDENT

Mr. NUNES. Thank you, Mr. Blackman. As I stated in the beginning, I don't mean to be hardline about this, but we do have all of your statements for the record, and it is very important that we do limit the statements to 5 minutes, and at this point, I will drop the gavel at 5 minutes, because we have Members of Congress here who have questions, and we want to be able to ask questions and at any time we could be pulled to the Floor. So the quicker that we can get through the testimony, the more question and answer time that we can have. And so—and I am just doing this I think just so we can speed this along to make the hearing more effective.

So, with that, Mr. Martin, I will recognize you for 5 minutes.

STATEMENT OF JAMES MARTIN, EXECUTIVE DIRECTOR, UNITED SOUTH AND EASTERN TRIBES, INC., NASHVILLE, TENNESSEE

Mr. MARTIN. Thank you, Chairman Nunes.

USET has provided written testimony. We would like that submitted for the record. I would make some brief oral comments.

Mr. NUNES. Thank you.

Mr. MARTIN. I would make some brief oral comments.

Mr. NUNES. Thank you.

Mr. MARTIN. Chairman Nunes and other distinguished members of the National Park Subcommittee, we thank you for giving United South and Eastern Tribes an opportunity to testify on the discussion draft of the proposed amendments to the National Historic Preservation Act.

My name is James T. Martin. I am an enrolled member of the Poarch Band of Creek Indians. I am the executive director of the United South and Eastern tribes, an inter-tribal organization representing 24 federally recognized Indian tribes from Maine to Texas.

My testimony today will focus on Section 4 of the discussion draft, which proposes a change in the scope of historic properties subject to the Section 106 review process of the Historic Preservation Act.

In particular, Section 4 would eliminate the current language in Section 106 that includes as covered properties not only properties listed on the National Register, but also properties eligible for inclusion in the National Register, as virtually every tribal historic property falls into the latter category.

The termination of this category would essentially eliminate tribal sacred sites from the Section 106 process. Not only would tribes no longer be consulted when a Federal undertaking puts one of their sacred sites at risk, but the Federal agencies would no longer even be obligated to watch out for the sites.

Section 4 represents a draconian measure that will strike at the of tribal identity, severely undermining the progress made by the tribes in recent years to have their sacred sites respected and protected, and would represent the single worst piece of legislation for tribal culture since the infamous General Allotment Act of 1887, in which two-thirds of tribal reservation lands was submitted to non-Indian settlements.

In the National Historic Preservation Act, Congress specifically found that historic properties significant to the Nation's heritage are being lost or substantially altered often inadvertently with increasing frequency.

This inadvertent damage was done particularly where properties were not recognized historic essential, those properties were not listed on the National Register.

To address the fact, the National Register is not a comprehensive listing of historic properties.

Congress logically provided that the Act would also protect properties that are eligible for inclusion on the National Register.

Morever, due to historic problems of widespread looting and sale of Indian grave goods and artifacts, many of the tribes do not want their sites listed on publicly available lists. Yet, these sites are still deserving of the protection under the Act.

In 1992, Congress amended the Act to ensure the protection of tribal properties of cultural and religious significance.

Congress established two requirements: First, the Act obligates a Federal agency to evaluate its undertaking for their impact on tribal historic properties. Second, the Act obligates the Federal agency to seek official tribal views through consultation on the effects of the consultation.

Notably, the Act only provides tribes with the right to consult. After a Federal agency has engaged in tribal consultation, it is free to pursue whatever course it deems best, even if that course is opposed by an affected tribe.

In that sense, the tribal rights in the Act are actually quite limited in scope. Nevertheless, the Act in genl and Section 106 in particular is relied upon by tribes throughout the United States to give them a place at the table when Federal action jeopardizes tribal sacred sites.

The tribal constitution rights in the Act are derived from general principles of Federal Indian law, which recognizes tribal sovereignty, places the tribal U.S. relationship in a government-to-government framework, and establishes a trust responsibility to Indian tribes.

The proposed amendment would be contrary to those principles.

And notably, at least 95 percent of the history of America occurred prior to 1492. That history is recorded in the sites of our cultural and religious importance to our tribes.

Although USET strongly opposes Section 4 of this discussion draft, USET is open to working with the Subcommittee and other interested parties, in finding ways to address the underlying needs of developers, including notably the telecommunication industry so long as the solution does not jeopardize sacred sites or the rights of tribes to be consulted when a Federal agency acts in a manner which could adversely affect a tribal sacred site.

Again, Mr. Chairman, I thank you for this opportunity to talk to the Subcommittee, and USET looks forward to working with this committee as we study this matter and approach it in a manner that is sensitive to the rights and the laws that have been passed to protect our tribal sacred sites. Thank you, sir.

[The prepared statement of Mr. Martin follows:

**Statement of James T. Martin, Executive Director,
United South and Eastern Tribes, Inc.**

Introduction. Chairman Nunes and members of the National Parks Subcommittee, my name is James T. Martin. I am a member of the Poarch Band of Creek Indians and Executive Director of the United South and Eastern Tribes, Inc.

(USET), an inter-tribal organization representing 24 tribes from Maine to Texas. USET appreciates this opportunity to provide testimony on the discussion draft of proposed amendments to the National Historic Preservation Act (NHPA). We especially appreciate that you are providing this opportunity before any actual legislation has been introduced. Such early consultation between the Federal Government and tribes on Federal actions that will significantly affect tribes is in the best traditions of the government-to-government relationship and is consistent with the Federal trust responsibility.

My testimony will focus on Section 4 of the discussion draft, which proposes a change in the scope of historic properties subject to the Federal consultation obligation found in Section 106 of the NHPA ("the Section 106 process"). In particular, Section 4 would eliminate the current language in Section 106 that includes as covered properties not only properties listed on the National Register, but also properties "eligible for inclusion in the National Register." As virtually every tribal historic property, defined in the NHPA as properties of "religious and cultural importance" to a tribe or Native Hawaiian Organization, falls into this latter category, the termination of this category would essentially eliminate tribal sacred sites from the Section 106 process. As such, Section 4 represents a draconian measure that would strike at the heart of tribal identity, severely undermine the progress made by tribes in recent years to have our sacred places respected and protected, and would represent the single worst piece of legislation for tribal culture since the infamous General Allotment Act of 1887, which resulted in the loss of two-thirds of tribal reservation lands to non-Indian settlement.

At least 95% of the history of the Americas occurred before 1492 when Columbus happened upon this continent. That history is recorded in the sites of cultural and religious importance to tribes. That history should be accorded a weight equal to that given historic properties of far more recent vintage.

Notwithstanding USET's objections to Section 4, USET is willing to work with the Subcommittee and other interested parties to find ways to address the Subcommittee's concerns. USET has worked on these issues intensely for several years in the context of the development by the Federal Communications Commission of a Nationwide Programmatic Agreement (NPA) implementing the Section 106 process. During that proceeding, USET put a number of proposals on the table for consideration by both the FCC and the telecommunications industry. The telecommunications industry was generally not willing to engage USET in a substantive way and sought to sharply limit tribal rights in the NPA. The FCC took on the difficult role of Solomon and adopted a balanced document that, while it did not give USET all it wanted, at least assured that the tribal voice would continue to be heard when a tribal site was at risk. In a corollary document known as the Best Practices, USET agreed to a voluntary process whereby the tribal right of consultation with the FCC could be waived when industry had worked with an affected tribe to resolve siting issues. Though never properly appreciated by industry, this waiver was a huge concession by USET made in the name of finding a workable solution to industry's concerns while still assuring that tribal sites and rights were maintained. USET also agreed to participate in and strongly supported the development by the FCC of the Tower Construction Notification System, a database that would electronically alert telecommunications companies of areas of cultural interest to tribes. Through this database, industry can quickly identify what tribes they need to contact in any given area based upon their site locations. Consequently, through this tribal self-identification the number of tribes needing to be contacted will be greatly reduced. Already, over 300 tribes have entered their areas of cultural interest into the database. This extraordinary response by tribes demonstrates our commitment to assisting industry with solutions to their concerns.

Although USET did not find industry a willing partner in our efforts to craft solutions that benefit both parties, as a matter of principle we remain open to working with all parties and will continue to extend an invitation to industry to work with us, rather than against us, to assure the efficient development of a universal communications infrastructure without compromising the sacred heritage of America's first peoples.

The National Historic Preservation Act provides critical protection for tribal sacred sites. The National Historic Preservation Act (NHPA) provides protection for "districts, sites, buildings, structures and objects significant in American history, architecture, archeology, engineering, and culture." 16 U.S.C. Section 440(f). The NHPA does this by requiring federal agencies engaged in a "federal undertaking" to "take into account the effect" the undertaking may have on historic properties "included", or "eligible for inclusion" in the National Register of Historic Places. Id.

The NHPA defines "Undertaking" as "a project, activity, or program funded in whole or in part under the direct or indirect jurisdiction of a Federal agency, including—(A) those carried out by or on behalf of the agency; (B) those carried out with Federal financial assistance; (C) those requiring a Federal permit, license, or approval; and, (D) those subject to State or local regulation administered pursuant to a delegation or approval by a Federal agency." 16 U.S.C. 470w(7).

The NHPA is implemented through a set of regulatory requirements commonly referred to as the Section 106 process, a consultation process through which federal agencies collect information concerning a particular site's eligibility for the National Register, potential adverse effects the undertaking may have on the site, and ways to mitigate any adverse effects. See 34 C.F.R. Part 800.

The NHPA sets forth two distinct requirements with regard to Tribes. First, the NHPA obligates a Federal agency to evaluate its undertakings for their impact on tribal historic properties. 16 U.S.C. 470a(d)(6)(A). In carrying out this obligation, a Federal agency would, in many cases, need to secure the cultural and religious expertise of any Tribe whose historic property could be affected. This is necessary in order to properly evaluate the impact of that undertaking on that Tribe's historic property.

Second, a Federal agency is obligated to seek official tribal views through consultation on the effect of an undertaking, a distinctly different exercise from securing the Tribe's cultural and religious expertise for evaluating the impact of an undertaking. Specifically, the NHPA provides that federal agencies "shall consult with any Indian tribe and Native Hawaiian organization that attaches religious or cultural significance" to properties that might be affected by a federal undertaking. 16 U.S.C. Section 470a(d)(6)(B) (emphasis added).

Notably, the NHPA only provides tribes with a right to be consulted. After a Federal agency has engaged in tribal consultation, it is free to pursue whatever course it deems best even if that course is one opposed by an affected tribe. In that sense, the tribal rights in the NHPA are actually quite limited in scope. Nonetheless, the Section 106 process is relied upon by tribes throughout the United States to give them a voice.

The Section 106 process embodies quintessentially American values that should not be undermined. In the best traditions of American democracy the Section 106 process gives marginalized groups a role in the shaping of the American identity by assuring them a voice when their own interests are jeopardized. Without this process, tribes would be virtually powerless to act to protect their heritage. In some ways the NHPA itself is an historical marker of American identity and, as such, should not be weakened.

Of course, Congress was specifically thinking about American values when it enacted the NHPA declaring in Section 1 that

"(1) the spirit and direction of the Nation are founded upon and reflected in its historic heritage;

(2) the historical and cultural foundations of the Nation should be preserved as a living part of our community life and development in order to give a sense of orientation to the American people;

(3) historic properties significant to the Nation's heritage are being lost or substantially altered, often inadvertently, with increasing frequency;

(4) the preservation of this irreplaceable heritage is in the public interest so that its vital legacy of cultural, educational, aesthetic, inspirational, economic, and energy benefits will be maintained and enriched for future generations of Americans;"

These statements ring with the greatness of America, but it would be a hollow ring if they were not applied to the historic properties of all Americans. In the NHPA, Congress has truly recognized the value of the meaning of American history; that the history of all communities is worthy of respect; that the lessons of the past can inform the actions of the present and future; that historic properties of all types represent a priceless heritage whose loss cannot be mitigated.

In the interests of justice, Section 106 should be strengthened, not weakened, by giving tribes more than just consultation rights. Section 106 only provides tribes a consultation right. This right is very limited in scope. A Federal agency after review and consultation with an affected tribe, can choose to ignore the tribal views and proceed with a particular action. Since 1492, Indian tribes within what is now the United States have, as a group, lost 98% of their aboriginal land base. This percentage is even higher for the member tribes of USET, whose aboriginal lands were the first to be subsumed in the process of European settlement. Today, as a result, the overwhelming majority of tribal properties of cultural and religious significance are located off Indian Reservations and Federal trust lands and therefore lie beyond tribal control. The National Historic Preservation Act (NHPA) recognizes the validity of continuing tribal concerns with the protection of both on- and off-Reservation properties of cultural and religious significance, and

establishes, through Section 106, extensive Federal agency consultation requirements with tribes when there is a Federal "undertaking" with the potential to have
any affect on such properties. Sometimes, however, a consultation right is just so
much hot air. This Committee should consider giving tribes the ability in certain
situations to halt a Federal action that threatens a significant tribal cultural or religious property.

**The telecommunications industry, which appears to be a strong advocate
for Section 4 of the discussion draft, has consistently advocated for weak-
ening tribal consultation rights under Section 106.** Over the last three years,
USET has been intensely involved in the development and promulgation of a Nationwide Programmatic Agreement (NPA) by the Federal Communications Commission. The NPA replaces the NHPA regulations, providing a customized process for
Section 106 consultation with regard to the siting of communications towers. USET
was extremely interested in this document because, despite the NHPA, literally tens
of thousands of cell towers have been constructed and received FCC broadcasting
licenses with virtually no effort by the FCC to consult with tribes. One can see
major sacred mountains in the Southwest that look like porcupines because of the
antenna farms that have been placed upon them without any tribal consultation.

In a belated attempt to make up for past errors, the FCC at one point stated that
it had delegated its consultation obligations to the cell tower companies, who subse-
quently began sending letters to tribes demanding information, some of it very sensitive in nature, and asserting that if the information was not provided within a certain timeframe, usually 10 to 30 days, as one typical letter to the Chitimacha Tribe
of Louisiana put it, "[w]e will presume that a lack of response from the Chitimacha
Tribe of Louisiana to this letter will indicate that the Chitimacha Tribe of Louisiana
has concluded that the particular project is not likely to affect sacred tribal resources." Tribes have literally received thousands of these letters. To add insult to
injury, the letters frequently refer to the tribes as "organizations" or "groups" dem-
onstrating a lack of respect for tribal sovereignty, ignorance of the status of tribes
and their unique legal rights, and generally conveying an impression that these
companies do not care about tribal views. The Tribal Historic Preservation Officer
for the Mississippi Band of Choctaw Indians, Kenneth H. Carleton, has noted that
the Mississippi Band had received "a minimum of over 1,000 requests" from cell
tower companies, many providing virtually no information on the location of the
sites or maps, but all with at least a check off saying that there are no sites of religious or cultural importance to the tribe to make it easy to for tribes to "rubber
stamp their requests."

The major telecommunications companies were involved early in the NPA's development (far earlier than tribes). The telecommunications companies raised their
issues including a desire to complete historic reviews quickly, at a minimum cost,
and with certainty. In those efforts they sought to shove aside tribal concerns. While
acknowledging on the one-hand the unique status of Indian tribes, the companies
on the other hand would essentially argue that that unique status should not result
in any actual difference in how tribal interests are treated.

The industry position is understandable. They are for-profit entities. Conducting
historic property reviews, although only a fraction of the cost of constructing a
tower, does have a cost (of course, the destruction of a sacred site cannot be meas-
ured in monetary terms). However, when the FCC licenses a tower, it is essentially
granting a license to these companies to make money. As one industry ad with a
photo of a cell tower put it: "This is not a cell tower. This is a money tree." As industry stands to benefit greatly from FCC licensing, it should also bear the cost of assuring the protection of historic properties. Congress has weighed the competing values of keeping costs low for developers and telecommunications companies, with the
imperative of preserving our national heritage. The result of that deliberation provided tribes with consultation rights, a boon to tribes, but not with veto rights, a
boon to federal agencies and developers.

**USET has sought to work closely with Industry, which has been a very
reluctant partner in seeking solutions that protect tribal consultation
rights regarding sacred sites.** Almost four years ago, USET entered into detailed
negotiations with a communications industry association to develop a process for addressing these issues that worked for both industry and tribes. USET recognizes
that the construction of a universal wireless telecommunications infrastructure network is vital to the economic and social future of the United States. However, the
tribal interests at issue are also vital, both to the tribes, and to the United States
in terms of its historic preservation goals and its national identity as a nation of
diverse and vibrant peoples and cultures. USET worked hard to find pragmatic solutions, while still assuring respect for tribal sovereignty and maintaining the FCC's
ultimate consultation responsibility. Based on the negotiations, USET developed and

sent to the industry group a set of protocols. We waited many months for a response, and then were told that the industry group had no further interest in these negotiations.

This experience told us that it is vital that the Federal government, consistent with its trust responsibility, assure that the tribal voice is heard. USET knows, from other Section 106 negotiations, that tribal concerns can be addressed without undermining the mission of a federal agency. For example, USET tribes have successfully negotiated a Memorandum of Agreement with the Mississippi National Guard, which among other things protects a tribal sacred site in the middle of a tank training range. Both sides made compromises to ensure that the vital interests of both could be protected. Similarly, the Louisiana tribes have a memorandum of agreement with the Louisiana National Guard. When an issue arose regarding rerouting a dangerous road at Camp Beauregard through an archeological site, the Louisiana Indian tribes worked with the Louisiana National Guard to permit the rerouting after appropriate archeological excavation and mitigation was undertaken. Tribes are not irrational; they have the same interests and concerns as do other communities. They want to build a solid working relationship with industry to assure that everybody's interests are given due regard.

The current definition of properties covered under Section 106 of the NHPA is the only sensible definition. The National Historic Preservation Act defines "'historic property' or 'historic resource'" as "any prehistoric or historic district, site, building, structure, or object included in, or eligible for inclusion on the National Register, including artifacts, records, and material remains related to such a property or resource." 16 U.S.C. Sec. 470w(5) (emphasis added). Congress found that "historic properties significant to the Nation's heritage are being lost or substantially altered, often inadvertently, with increasing frequency." 16 U.S.C. Sec. 470(b)(3) (emphasis added). This inadvertent damage was done principally where properties were not recognized as historic; essentially those properties not listed in the National Register of Historic Places. To address the fact that the National Register is not a comprehensive listing of historic properties, Congress logically provided that the NHPA would also protect properties that are "eligible for inclusion on the National Register"."

The NHPA authorizes the creation of one list of properties—the National Register (16 U.S.C. Sec. 470a), but as is evident from the definition of "historic property," the NHPA specifically protects properties both on the National Register as well as properties not on the National Register if they meet National Register criteria. The Advisory Council on Historic Preservation, in its implementing regulations, recognized the NHPA's mandate, and therefore Congress' mandate, to protect all eligible properties and provided that the term "eligible for inclusion in the National Register includes both properties formally determined as such in accordance with regulations of the Secretary of the Interior and all other properties that meet the National Register criteria." 36 C.F.R. Part 800.16(l)(2). In this definition, the Advisory Council was recognizing that the Department of the Interior has created a second list of properties that have been formally determined to be eligible for, but are not on, the National Register. However, that second list is not comprehensive and is essentially merely an aid to implementing the NHPA. Therefore, consistent with the language of the statute, the Advisory Council did not limit its definition just to Interior's "eligibility" list, but also included all eligible properties. The Advisory Council understands that there are many sites that have not yet been evaluated but that will be found eligible for the National Register. Such sites would be in great peril if there were no requirement to essentially "watch out" for them and protect them where they are found.

Due to the historic problem of widespread looting and sale of Indian grave goods and artifacts, many tribes do not want their sites identified on a publicly availabl e list. These tribes still expect and are entitled to the full protections of the NHPA from Federal undertakings that could damage these sites. However, these tribes are not interested in seeing their sacred sites placed on publicly available lists, including the National Register.

General principles of Federal Indian law recognize tribal sovereignty, place Tribal-U.S. relations in a government-to-government framework, and establish a Federal trust responsibility to Indian tribes. These general principles are rooted in the U.S. Constitution (Art. I, Section 8), Federal case law, Federal statutes, Presidential Executive Orders, regulations, and case law, as well as in the policy statement of the Advisory Council on Historic Preservation entitled The Council's Relationship with Indian Tribes. As such they form the basis for the tribal consultation rights in the NHPA. To delete those rights would be to undermine the entire structure of Federal Indian law and tribal sovereignty.

Congressional Indian policy with respect to Indian religious matters is set forth in the American Indian Religious Freedom Act (AIRFA):

"Protection and preservation of traditional religions of Native Americans

Henceforth it shall be the policy of the United States to protect and preserve for American Indians their inherent right of freedom to believe, express, and exercise the traditional religions of the American Indian, Eskimo, Aleut, and Native Hawaiians, including but not limited to access to sites, use and possession of sacred objects, and the freedom to worship through ceremonials and traditional rites."

42 U.S.C. Section 1996. AIRFA also requires federal agencies to consult with Native American traditional religious leaders in order to evaluate existing policies and procedures and make changes necessary to preserve Native American cultural practices. Act of Aug. 11, 1978, P.L. 95-341, Section 2. 92 Stat. 470.

There are several other statutes where Congress has set forth a policy of protecting traditional Indian religion, such as the Native American Graves Protection and Repatriation Act (NAGPRA, 25 U.S.C. §3001 et.seq.), the Archaeological Resources Protection Act (ARPA, 16 U.S.C. §470aa-70mm), and the National Museum of the American Indian Act (20 U.S.C. §80q et.seq.). The consultation requirements of, and legal rights established by, these statutes are not geographically confined to situations where cultural or religious objects are found (or activities occur) solely on tribal lands.

There are several presidential orders that mandate Federal consultation with Indian tribes. Executive Order 13007 (May, 24 1996) (hereafter "Executive Order on Sacred Sites") directs federal agencies to provide access to American Indian sacred sites, to protect the physical integrity of such sites and, where appropriate, to maintain the confidentiality of these sites. This Executive Order on Sacred Sites also incorporates a prior Executive Memorandum issued on April 29, 1994, which directed federal agencies to establish policies and procedures for dealing with Native American Tribal Governments on a "government-to-government basis."

Executive Order 13175 (Consultation and Coordination with Indian Tribes, November 6, 2000) directs Federal officials to establish regular and meaningful consultation and collaboration with tribal officials in the development of Federal policies that have tribal implications.

The Federal Courts have developed canons of construction that are used to interpret Indian treaties and statutes relating to Indians. The fundamental component of these canons of construction is that treaties and statutes are to be liberally interpreted to accomplish their protective purposes, with any ambiguities to be resolved in the favor of the Indian tribes or individual Indians. See Alaska Pacific Fisheries Co. V. United States, 248 U.S. 78, 89 (1918) ("the general rule [is] that statutes passed for the benefit of the dependent Indian tribes or communities are to be liberally construed, doubtful expressions being resolved in favor of the Indians"); Tulee v. Washington, 315 U.S. 681, 684-685 (1942); Carpenter v. Shaw, 280 U.S. 363 (1930); McClanahan v. Arizona State Tax Com'n, 411 U.S. 164 (1973). In this context, the National Historic Preservation Act should be read broadly to support and protect tribal interests.

Conclusion. Although USET strongly opposes Section 4 of the discussion draft, USET is open to working with the Subcommittee and other interested parties in finding ways to address the underlying needs of developers, including notably the telecommunications industry, so long as any solution does not jeopardize tribal sacred sites or the rights of tribes to be consulted when a Federal agency acts in a manner which could adversely affect a tribal sacred site. USET thanks the Subcommittee for this opportunity to testify and looks forward to working closely with you and your staff to find practical solutions that protect tribal sites and rights, while addressing the concerns of all the stakeholders in the Section 106 process.

Mr. NUNES. Thank you, Mr. Martin. Mr. Altschul, you are recognized for 5 minutes.

STATEMENT OF MICHAEL ALTSCHUL, SR., VICE PRESIDENT AND GENERAL COUNSEL, CTIA, THE WIRELESS ASSOCIATION, WASHINGTON, D.C.

Mr. ALTSCHUL. Well, thank you, Mr. Chairman, and members of the Subcommittee for the opportunity to testify on behalf of the wireless industry concerning the National Historic Preservation Act and the Subcommittee's discussion draft proposal to amend the Act.

My name is Michael Altschul and I am CTIA's general counsel. CTIA's president, Steve Largent, wanted to be here today, but he is getting over a minor health problem. Steve asked me to voice his support for the approach taken in Section 4 of the discussion draft, and he also wants you to know that he looks forward to working with the Committee, tribes, and other interested parties on this issue.

While other industries were the primary focus of the Act, cellular service didn't exist 40 years ago when created the Act, I am here to talk about the impact of this law on the wireless industry and how Congress can provide much needed certainty to the National Historic Preservation Act's Section 106 review process.

First, I want to emphasize that the wireless industry is committed to preserving our Nation's cultural heritage, including sites of religious and cultural importance to tribes and Native Hawaiian organizations. Wireless companies are proud of their success in balancing the dual aims of historic preservation and the siting of wireless towers. These goals are not mutually exclusive. We acknowledge that the lessons learned from the NPA and Best Practices Agreement, and we welcome the opportunity to consult with tribes to protect sites of religious and cultural significance.

Second, it is critical to understand that without antennas, there are no wireless services. Wireless carriers must install new facilities to extend coverage to unserved or underserved areas. If a carrier is delayed building a tower, customers are deprived of the ability to make and receive wireless calls in that community, including emergency calls to 911.

Similarly, if a carrier is unable to construct a new cell site or collocate its wireless facilities on an existing tower to accommodate new subscribers and increased demand, all of its customers will experience dropped or blocked calls due to congestion.

Third, as a general rule, wireless carriers require local zoning consent to construct new towers. The local zoning process involves public participation and historic preservation experts can and do participate in the review of tower siting proposals.

The wireless industry routinely accommodates local concerns by minimizing the visual impact of wireless antennas. Since a picture is worth a thousand words, we have brought two examples to show the Committee of the efforts the industry takes to accommodate the impact of these facilities.

Even though the Federal Communications Commission does not review or approve the siting of wireless towers—and doesn't even track the location of most towers—the FCC has taken the position that the siting of any new tower by a wireless carrier is a Federal undertaking subject to Section 106 review.

This means a separate Federal process exists even where the local government has heard from and considered the views of its citizens and historic preservation experts.

In some cases, parties have pursued a National Historic Preservation Act review following approval by the local zoning board, denial of their appeal by the courts and even when the owner of the

property did not favor designation on the National Register and
supported construction of the tower.

While there is no dispute that the National Historic Preservation
Act requires review of Federal undertakings on properties included
or eligible for inclusion in the National Register, the definition of
what is ineligible property has strayed from what Congress intended, creating controversy and uncertainty for wireless carriers,
tower owners, agencies, historic groups, and the public.

While there are registries and other resources wireless carriers
can and do consult to identify whether properties have been included or nominated for inclusion in the National Register, many
stakeholders have taken the position that the industry must consider any property that could conceivably meet the National Register criteria—potentially, any property over 50 years old, even if
no steps had ever been taken to nominate the property for inclusion in the National Register.

Under this approach, the meaning and scope of Section 106 has
been vastly expanded in a way that virtually ignores the National
Register itself and renders the nomination process and listing on
that exclusive role irrelevant for purposes of the Section 106 review
process.

In 2003, Chairman Pombo and then Subcommittee Chairman
Radanovich recognized this problem in a letter to the ACHP, noting
that the number of properties that meet the National Register criteria is unknowable, probably in the many tens of millions, and
urging that the Section 106 process return to the carefully defined
scope originally intended by Congress. CTIA agrees, and believes it
would be more rational and more consistent with the intent of Congress to provide a concrete definition of eligibility that offers a clear
path for wireless carriers to satisfy their National Historic Preservation Act obligations in a way that is sensitive to historic preservation concerns while providing certainty for wireless service development. That is why we endorse the approach taken in Section 4
of the discussion draft, and why we think this clarification is of
critical importance.

Mr. Chairman, thank you for the opportunity to testify this
morning. I look forward to answering any questions you or the
members may have.

[The prepared statement of Mr. Altschul follows:]

Statement of Michael F. Altschul, Senior Vice President and General Counsel, CTIA—The Wireless Association

Chairman Nunes, Ranking Member Kildee, and members of the Subcommittee,
thank you for the invitation to testify on the National Historic Preservation Act
("NHPA"). Protecting historic and culturally sensitive landmarks benefits our Nation, and the wireless industry is committed to preserving our cultural heritage.
CTIA member companies work closely with local communities to balance the dual
aims of historic preservation and the siting of wireless towers to keep pace with
public demand for wireless communications services. These goals are not mutually
exclusive, and I appreciate the opportunity to appear today on behalf of the wireless
industry.

Let me preface my remarks by noting the public's ever-growing demand for wireless service. Wireless communications have become an integral part of the daily
lives of Americans and the American economy. Today, more than 182 million Americans subscribe to wireless services—in fact, there are more mobile devices in the
United States than traditional telephone access lines. Not only are wireless devices
now omnipresent, but Americans are increasingly relying on their wireless service—

average minutes of use increased to 596 minutes per month in 2004, a 14% increase over 2003. With respect to public demand, CTIA members hear their customers loud and clear: they want reliable service, with an ever expanding service area, and an array of new applications and offerings. And nowhere is this more relevant than in our Nation's rural areas as wireless service promises to be a key platform to bridge the digital divide.

Wireless service, moreover, plays an important role in public safety as wireless callers make more than 200,000 911 calls every day, seeking emergency assistance from police, fire, and emergency medical personnel. In addition, local, state, and federal agencies increasingly rely on wireless services to carry out their emergency public safety and homeland security responsibilities.

Antennas and the towers upon which antennas are hung—commonly referred to as "base stations" or "cell sites"—are absolutely essential to meeting the public demand for commercial wireless services and the needs of our Nation's first responders. Indeed, if spectrum is considered the "lifeblood" of wireless service, then towers and antennas are the critical arteries and capillaries that deliver wireless services across this great land. While the media often highlight exciting new applications such as camera phones or mobile networks' ability to deliver video broadcasts, it is the bricks and mortar of basic construction projects (i.e., antenna siting) that deliver services to American consumers. For example, a wireless carrier must install new facilities each time it wants to extend its coverage to an unserved or underserved area. If a carrier is delayed in building a tower in the new area, customers are deprived of the ability to make and receive calls in that community. Similarly, if a carrier is unable to construct a new cell site or collocate its wireless facilities on an existing tower to relieve congestion, customers will experience dropped or blocked calls (including E911 call attempts).

I am here today to talk about the impact of the National Historic Preservation Act on the wireless industry—and specifically, how Congress can provide much needed certainty to the NHPA review process, commonly referred to as the section 106 process. As you know, the section 106 process requires federal agencies to determine whether their undertakings could adversely affect a historic property included in, or eligible for inclusion in, the National Register of Historic Places. Tower siting is subject to NHPA because the Federal Communications Commission ("FCC") takes the position that the siting of any new tower by a wireless carrier is a "federal" undertaking subject to section 106 review—even though the FCC does not review and approve the siting of wireless towers and in fact for most towers, the FCC does not even know where the tower is located. Subjecting wireless carriers to this cumbersome compliance process is particularly burdensome because of the number of towers needed to meet the public demand for wireless services. CTIA believes that Congress can act here to maintain the integrity of our Nation's historic preservation policies while limiting unnecessary delays and providing finality to the tower siting approval process.

By way of background, although Congress recognized that mobile services are nationwide in nature, it explicitly determined that local governments—not the federal government—should oversee and authorize the placement, construction and modification of wireless towers. Indeed, Congress could not have been more specific in vesting the regulation of wireless tower siting with local and state government zoning authorities, subject only to the specific limitations included in the 1996 amendments to the Communications Act. Today, in nearly every instance a wireless carrier cannot construct a new radio tower without local zoning board consent, which involves a wide variety of factors including consideration of potential impacts on historic properties. The local zoning process involves public participation, and historic preservation experts can and do participate in review of tower siting proposals.

As a result of section 106, a separate, federal process exists—involving the Advisory Council on Historic Preservation ("ACHP"), State Historic Protection Officers ("SHPOs"), Tribal Historic Preservation Officers ("THPOs"), Tribes, historic groups, and the public—in a review of the historical and cultural impact of proposed towers. The parties have generally recognized that the scope of this review for wireless tower siting has become unwieldy in recent years. With the FCC's participation, a 2001 Collocation Agreement was enacted to limit NHPA review of the placement of antennas on existing towers and buildings or other non-tower structures in specific circumstances. And in 2004, a Nationwide Programmatic Agreement ("the 2004 NPA") was adopted in an effort to clarify and streamline the section 106 review process. Several significant issues, however, still remain.

As you may know, CTIA has asked the U.S. Court of Appeals for the D.C. Circuit to review whether wireless tower siting constitutes a "federal undertaking" subject to section 106 review. Notably, two FCC Commissioners, including the new Chairman, dissented from the FCC Order adopting the 2004 NPA, concluding that wireless tower siting is not a federal undertaking. However, I am not here today to address the undertaking issue but instead to raise a fundamental aspect of the NHPA section 106 review—what makes a property "eligible" for inclusion in the National Register, i.e., which properties require section 106 investigation and review by wireless carriers seeking to site an antenna.

The NHPA requires review of federal undertakings on properties included or "eligible for inclusion" in the National Register. For years, the definition of eligible properties has strayed from what Congress intended, creating controversy and uncertainty for wireless carriers, tower owners, agencies, historic groups and the public. While there are registries and other resources wireless carriers can consult to identify whether properties have been included or nominated for inclusion in the National Register, the FCC, the ACHP, SHPOs, and historic groups have taken the position that the industry must consider any property that could conceivably meet the National Register criteria—potentially any property over 50 years old (a universe of properties that could run into the millions)—even if no steps had ever been taken to nominate the property for inclusion in the National Register. Under this approach, the meaning and scope of section 106 has been vastly expanded in a way that virtually ignores the National Register itself and renders the nomination process and listing on that exclusive roll irrelevant for purposes of the section 106 review process. In some cases, parties have pursued NHPA review following approval by the local zoning board and even when the owner of the property in question did not favor designation on the National Register and supported construction of the tower.

As a result of this overly broad interpretation, wireless carriers routinely must investigate an uncertain universe of potentially eligible properties in a several mile radius from the proposed site. This causes significant delay, additional costs, and uncertainty in the tower siting process. And delay, added costs, uncertainty, and lack of finality are not merely hypothetical—in the end, certain areas are unserved or without adequate coverage for far too long, to the detriment of American consumers. A few examples follow:

- In rural Georgia, a carrier identified an initial site for a proposed tower but was directed by the SHPO to seek another location because a nearby property was old enough to be considered eligible for the National Register. The SHPO provided guidance with respect to the replacement site. Upon submission to the SHPO, the carrier was informed that the new site was too close to another potentially eligible property. These iterative attempts to avoid potentially "eligible" sites delayed the project by a nearly half a year at a cost of $30,000.00. A site acceptable to the SHPO has still not been located. As a result, the carrier is reassessing whether it will be able to provide service to the area. The delay and cost incurred in serial attempts to find an acceptable site can do more than delay new service, it can cause a carrier to consider abandoning its plans to provide service to the area.

- In upstate New York, the SHPO decided that construction of a new tower would have an adverse effect on an historic property located over a mile away, which resulted in a four year delay in the construction of the tower. To view the tower from the property, one had to look through trees, across a busy highway, through utility lines strung along the highway, and then look more than a mile further. When the FCC examined the case it found that the SHPO's position was unpersuasive and authorized the construction of the tower. However, during the four year dispute, the public was deprived of increased coverage and enhanced service quality. Any adverse finding, regardless of merit, triggers significant delay.

- New Jersey's Garden State Parkway has recently been identified as eligible for listing in the National Register. This 2-to-6 lane restricted access toll highway has gaps in wireless service, and multiple towers are required for comprehensive wireless coverage, including the ability to make emergency 911 calls. Yet, proposed towers—which may be located on a nearby road and only momentarily visible when driving along the Parkway—will trigger a section 106 review process that can add more than six months to complete, requiring negotiation of a Memorandum of Agreement between the carrier, the SHPO, the FCC and potentially the ACHP, preparation and filing of an FCC submission, and expenditure of thousands of dollars. Thus, this process automatically produces delay in siting, resulting in public demand that goes unmet.

- In rural Mississippi a carrier has been advised by the SHPO that it could not locate a proposed tower because it was too close to several potentially eligible properties. Not only did the property owner and residents of the area disagree, but a tower had been approved by the SHPO and was constructed only 1000 feet from the proposed site. This site would have provided service to a town of barely 1,000 people.

- A farmstead owner and the SHPO in New York believe that a tower constructed in 1987 adversely affects the farmstead by changing the historic setting, even though the farmstead owner has constructed modern silos and other modern farm buildings on the property. The battle over the tower, which has been ongoing since 2000, has cost the carrier hundreds of thousands of dollars. This is just one example of where post-construction claims are entertained and can linger for years, upending finality and certainty in the siting tower siting process.
- NHPA proceedings and delay are not just inconvenient and costly, they can create serious threats to public safety. In rural western Maryland, a NHPA challenge to a tower proposed for both public safety and commercial wireless services resulted in a three year delay in construction. During the protracted proceedings, emergency services communications in the area became so degraded that Medivac helicopter pilots transporting patients to nearby hospitals could no longer communicate with EMS crews on the ground or hospitals. Concerned that the ability of its emergency teams to save lives was endangered, the State of Maryland requested expedited consideration, the FCC issued an order finding the tower posed no adverse effect to historic properties, and the tower was constructed.

As noted above, the expansive definition of properties eligible for inclusion increases the universe of properties that carriers must investigate and that can trigger reviews, causing delay and uncertainty. In 2003, Chairman Pombo and then-Subcommittee Chairman Radanovich recognized this problem in a letter to the ACHP, noting that the number of properties that meet the National Register criteria is unknowable—probably in the many tens of millions—and urging that the section 106 process return to the carefully defined scope originally intended by Congress.

The 2004 Nationwide Programmatic Agreement purported to provide more certainty to the eligible properties issue by directing the wireless industry to consult five specific sources of information to determine what properties nearby the site are "eligible for inclusion." At first glance, this may appear to be an improvement over the existing application of section 106. This modification, however, is illusory as it does not change the sweeping definition of properties eligible for inclusion. As a result, consultation with the five sources provides no safe harbor and no certainty for wireless carriers.

In addition, the 2004 NPA fails to provide finality once a wireless carrier completes its review of these sources. At any time, including while the tower is under construction or after it has been built, a party can interject a claim that an eligible property was overlooked—even if it does not appear in any of the five sources carriers are required to consult by the 2004 NPA. Further, the 2004 NPA creates a new petition process at the FCC that permits a party to allege an eligible property has been overlooked and allows the FCC to order construction halted, fine the wireless carrier or tower owner, and if the tower has been constructed, the FCC can order that it be demolished.

In essence, even following the 2004 Nationwide Programmatic Agreement, the NHPA section 106 review process remains completely open-ended, causing delays in the siting process and providing challengers an unending "second bite" opportunity to oppose sites that already have been approved by local zoning authorities. The result is a process that forces the wireless industry to make siting determinations that are forever subject to review and reversal. CTIA believes it would be more rational—and more consistent with Congress intent—to provide a concrete definition of eligibility that offers a clear path for wireless carriers to satisfy their NHPA obligations in a way that is sensitive to historic preservation concerns while providing certainty for wireless service deployment. Restoring significance to inclusion in the National Register and the nomination process for inclusion would eliminate hundreds of thousands of unnecessary identification and evaluation reviews of potentially eligible properties. Further, it would ensure that historic properties are properly reviewed within the section 106 process while eliminating an avoidable drain on resources.

Preserving historic sites and siting communications facilities to provide reliable wireless service are not mutually exclusive goals. CTIA urges Congress to restore clarity to the section 106 process and thereby remove the unnecessary delay, costs, and uncertainty from the tower siting process.

Mr. Chairman, thank you for the opportunity to testify this morning. I look forward to answering any questions you or the members may have.

Mr. NUNES. Thank you, Mr. Altschul. Ms. Wadhams, you are recognized for 5 minutes.

STATEMENT OF EMILY WADHAMS, VICE PRESIDENT, NATIONAL TRUST FOR HISTORIC PRESERVATION, WASHINGTON, D.C.

Ms. WADHAMS. Thank you, Mr. Chairman, and members of the Subcommittee for the opportunity to testify on behalf of the National Trust for Historic Preservation concerning the discussion draft proposal to amend the National Historic Preservation Act.

My name is Emily Wadhams, and I am the National Trust Vice President for Public Policy.

The National Trust and its preservation partners—organizations representing over 300,000 members—support the reauthorization of the Advisory Council on Historic Preservation as originally proposed by H.R. 3223 from the 108th Congress. We also support the reauthorization of the Historic Preservation Fund.

We strongly oppose, however, Sections 2, 3, and 4 of the discussion draft as changes that would substantially weaken the Preservation Act's core protections for historic properties, specifically Section 106.

The problems that apparently generated some of the proposed changes are fairly uncommon. There are numerous ways to deal with those concerns through administrative solutions. The Interstate Highway system exemption is a good example, and we see no need to take legislative approach to fix a program that generally works well.

Virtually every Congress since 1966 has worked to strengthen the Preservation Act because of the bipartisan consensus that saving America's heritage is a national goal. These discussion draft amendments threaten to alter that consensus. We are supportive of private property rights, but private property rights have never been allowed to take precedence over what is deemed to serve a greater public good, including the preservation of our national heritage.

Here are our principal concerns with the discussion draft.

First, Section 4. This is the most troubling provision to the preservation community because of the vast majority of historic places already known to be significant, they would be excluded from consideration under Section 106. It would limit the scope of Section 106 to historic properties in districts actually listed on the National Register. There are currently about 79,000 of these and also those determined by the Secretary to be eligible to, which adds about another 9,700 properties.

However, over the last 35 years, more than 350,000 historic properties have been determined eligible through the 106 reviews—about four times the number of those actually listed on the National Register, and they would be deprived of existing Federal safeguards.

Section 4 would also have serious consequences for elements of our heritage yet to be discovered and would give Federal agencies a free hand to plan projects that could harm historic places without any consideration of their significance.

And even more alarming, Section 4 would pose an immense thread to tribal historic resources and archaeological sites. Only a small fraction of traditional cultural properties have been listed or determined eligible.

The change in the law would threaten the destruction of the only clues we have into much of this Nation's past, including the 10,000 or so years worth of artifacts chronicling the history of the first Americans.

We have given numerous examples of this in our written testimony. What Americans consider to be significant is not static, and the beauty of the current eligibility language is that it allows for a dynamic public engagement process. A particular compelling case, as mentioned earlier, is the World Trade Center site. As a result of Section 106, the site was determined to be eligible for National Register, and only because of 106 was there a process for citizens, including the families of the victims to become engaged in the decisions regarding the redevelopment of that site.

This is just one of many examples, albeit a dramatic one, of how the process works on a daily basis to protect the places that have special meaning to us as Americans.

Section 2 of the discussion draft responds to the unusual situation of owner objection, and would prohibit eligibility determinations by the keeper if the owner objects to listing.

Owner objections are rare—only 15 in the last two years. This potential change is troubling for several reasons. In historic districts, it would ban eligibility determinations if more than 50 percent of the owners object and as a result all property owners within the district would lose the right to protect their property from potentially harmful Federal projects.

Furthermore, not recognizing the significance of a property by a determination of eligibility could negatively impact the Federal planning process for future 106 reviews.

And finally, Section 3 of the discussion draft would create a new requirement for certified local governments. It would dictate how those municipalities regulate their land use, even for projects with no Federal involvement.

No evidence is presented that this change is needed or will provide additional due process protections.

As exemplified by the President's Preserve America Executive Order, it is a civic responsibility and Federal obligation to ensure that vital historic resources are preserved for generations to come. We appreciate the Subcommittee holding a hearing to examine proposals outlined in the discussion draft, but urge you not to move forward with amendments that would undermine the integrity of the Preservation Act. Thank you for your time and your consideration of this important issue.

[The prepared statement of Ms. Wadhams follows:]

Statement of Emily Wadhams, Vice President for Public Policy, The National Trust for Historic Preservation

Thank you Mr. Chairman and members of the Subcommittee for this opportunity to testify on behalf of the National Trust for Historic Preservation concerning the National Historic Preservation Act (NHPA) and the Subcommittee's "discussion draft" proposal to amend the Act. The National Trust's President, Richard Moe, is out of the country this week and it was impossible for him to be here in person, but he has asked me to speak on his behalf and to convey his serious concerns about the importance of the issues raised by this draft.

For more than 50 years, the National Trust has been helping to protect the nation's heritage, as the Congressionally chartered leader of the private historic preservation movement in America. The National Trust, a nonprofit organization with more than a quarter million members throughout the country, is directly involved in saving the best of our past for future generations.

The National Trust and our partners in the historic preservation community support the reauthorization of the Advisory Council on Historic Preservation (ACHP)—as originally proposed by H.R. 3223 from the 108th Congress—and the reauthorization of the Historic Preservation Fund (HPF). We strongly oppose, however, Sections 2, 3, and 4 of the discussion draft that would substantially weaken the Preservation Act's fundamental core. We urge you to move forward in reauthorizing the ACHP and HPF, without including any amendments to the NHPA that would undermine the current safeguards for our nation's historic and archeological patrimony. Let me emphasize that the historic preservation community is absolutely united in our opposition to the amendments proposed in the discussion draft. As you know, the Trust joined six other national organizations in a joint letter to the Subcommittee—collectively representing this opposition on behalf of over 300,000 members and a wide variety of preservation advocates ranging from state and tribal officials to architects and archaeologists.

Historic preservation is the process of identifying places, sites and resources that have survived from our past; evaluating the meaning and value they have for us now; and keeping, using and caring for those significant places, sites and resources so they will survive into the future. The preamble to the NHPA, as passed by Congress in 1966, reminds us that "The spirit and direction of the nation are founded upon and reflected in its historic heritage;" and that "the historical and cultural foundations of the nation should be preserved as a living part of our community life and development in order to give a sense of orientation to the American people." Congress further clarified in 1980 that "the preservation of this irreplaceable heritage is in the public interest."

Virtually every Congress since 1966 has worked to strengthen the NHPA, because there has been a shared, bipartisan consensus that saving America's heritage should be, and has always been, a national goal. These discussion draft amendments, conversely, threaten to shatter that consensus. If enacted, they would represent by far the most serious threat to our heritage in the history of the Congress.

The problems that apparently generated the changes to Section 106 in the discussion draft are anecdotal and rare. Instead of developing strategic solutions to address those concerns, which could be accomplished entirely through the administrative process, this proposal vastly overreaches and would cause irreparable damage to historic properties nationwide by amending a federal law to satisfy a disgruntled minority. If the Subcommittee would like to develop responsible improvements to the Section 106 process, administrative mechanisms are available to accomplish this, such as the recent exemption of the Interstate Highway System and others.

The National Trust is firmly supportive of private property rights and advocates an appropriate balance between those rights and the greater public policy goals that benefit all citizens. In that regard, private property rights have never been allowed to take precedence over our shared national values and the preservation of our country's heritage. The Trust's own Congressional charter reflects the important role of private property ownership in our mission and greatly encourages active public participation in every facet of the historic preservation process.

The Preservation Act protects the rights and values of private property owners, local officials, and citizens across the United States, and gives them a place at the table when the actions of federal agencies threaten to affect their historic properties and their communities. Section 106 provides a process that requires those agencies to "take into account" the effects of their decisions and their projects on historic properties, and to work with states, tribes, and local communities to seek ways to lessen the effects of those projects. Section 106 requires a process, not an outcome. The goal is not to save every historic site but to make sure that they are considered and that their value is weighed against other public values. Section 106 helps to prevent governmental agencies from running roughshod over the rights of citizens, private property owners, local governments, and tribal governments when it comes to the protection of our American history.

- **The Discussion Draft Would Completely Eliminate From Section 106 Consideration Over Three Quarters of Currently Known Historic Properties that Have Already Been Determined Eligible for the National Register.**

Section Four of the discussion draft is the most troubling to us, because the vast majority of historic places already known to be significant would be excluded from consideration under Section 106. If this change were enacted, it would limit the scope of Section 106 to the 79,000 historic properties and districts actually listed on the National Register and those "determined by the Secretary to be eligible," which is about 9,700 additional properties. More than 350,000 historic properties, however, have been determined eligible by the SHPOs and federal agencies in the last 35 years through the Section 106 review process. While these determinations may be undisputed, they have not been reviewed by the Keeper of the National Register directly, and therefore, all of these known historic properties—more than four times the number of those listed on the National Register—would be deprived of existing federal safeguards.

- **The Discussion Draft Would Completely Eliminate the Requirement to Evaluate Significant Places that May Qualify for the National Register.**

Section Four would also have serious consequences for the elements of our heritage yet unknown or undiscovered. It would give federal agencies a free hand to plan projects that could harm or destroy historic places and archeological sites without even investigating their significance. Whether it is a century-old bridge that is a beloved community landmark, or a nineteenth century neighborhood that is threatened by a proposed highway, many of the places we treasure most in our communities have never even been evaluated for the Register. They would be stripped of any consideration under the discussion draft proposal. In order to protect their property from a federal undertaking, this change would place the burden on property owners themselves to pay for preparing a Register nomination at their own expense. To pursue the process all the way to the Keeper before the commencement of project planning process would be immensely difficult.

Section Four would pose an especially significant threat to tribal historic resources and archeological sites. Only a small fraction of the traditional cultural properties have been listed on the Register or determined eligible by the Keeper. The change in the law would threaten the destruction of the only clues we have into much of this nation's past—the 10,000 or so years' worth of artifacts chronicling pre-Columbian human history—a story that can only be discovered through the archeological record. Archaeological sites identified through the Section 106 process represent the historic spectrum ranging from the winter camp of Spanish explorer Coronado, the birthplace of southern patriot Robert Young Hayne, the African Burial Ground in Manhattan, the first Spanish settlement in St. Augustine, the Indian village adjacent to the 1607 Jamestown settlement, and many more. These chapters of our heritage might have been lost and destroyed had it not been for Section 106.

What Americans consider to be historic or culturally significant is not static, but is dynamic and evolving. When the Register was started, we tended to identify architecture or sites that told the stories of only the wealthiest or most famous Americans. The current Section 106 process now offers a process for protection of diverse historic resources. For example, the World Trade Center site in Lower Manhattan, where terrorists attacked the twin towers on September 11, 2001, has been recognized as eligible for the National Register, based on its extraordinary significance in our history. This site, where the lives of thousands of innocent Americans were lost, has become in a sense the Pearl Harbor of the 21st century, a place that affected the lives of every single one of us. As a result of Section 106, the World Trade Center site was evaluated for the Register and the public has had the opportunity to learn about significant elements at that location, some of which never would have been identified at all without the review process under current law. Because of Section 106, federally assisted projects such as the reconstruction of the commuter rail station at the World Trade Center have been significantly modified in response to consultation and will incorporate the preservation of elements within the site that will be visible to the public from the station. As an active participant in the Section 106 review process, the National Trust can assure the Subcommittee that, if the proposed amendments in the discussion draft had been in place, none of this ever would have happened. The World Trade Center is just one of many examples of how the current Section 106 process works on a daily basis to protect the places that have special meaning to us as Americans.

Section 110 of the Historic Preservation Act, and Section 3 of the "Preserve America" Executive Order signed by President Bush in 2003, direct federal agencies to inventory and evaluate their land holdings to determine what archeological or historical resources might be located on them. The discussion draft proposal would eliminate the incentive for federal agencies to evaluate their historic properties because a lack of information about their significance would be rewarded with an exemption from Section 106.

Federal agencies are required to investigate a whole variety of other types of resources prior to making decisions about their actions including the affects on wetlands, endangered species, groundwater, and soil. The long-standing requirement to investigate historic properties is no different from these other types of studies. By eliminating this requirement from Section 106, the proposal would single out historic places and relegate them to the status of second-class resources.

- **Section Two of the Discussion Draft Responds to an Uncommon Problem With a Needless and Draconian Remedy That Would Threaten Private Property Rights.**

Section Two of the discussion draft would prohibit eligibility determinations by the Keeper of the National Register if the owner objects to listing the property on the Register. Even historic properties and districts previously determined eligible by SHPOs or federal agencies could be prohibited from an eligibility determination by the Keeper under this provision.

In historic districts, this provision would ban eligibility determinations if more than 50 percent of the owners object within the district—or arguably, if any owners object. As a result, all property owners within the historic district would lose the right to protect their property from federal projects that could harm or destroy their communities. They would also lose incentives for private investment in the district generated by state and federal tax credits.

It is important for the Subcommittee to understand that owner objections to Register listing are very unusual; only 15 such objections have been raised nationwide in the last two years, even though the Subcommittee has been focusing attention on this issue. We strongly oppose amending the NHPA to address a circumstance that is so rare.

- **Section Three of the Discussion Draft Responds to an Uncommon Problem by Using Federal Law to Dictate Local Land Use Rules to Local Governments.**

Section Three, like Section Two, would respond to a virtually non-existent problem that is backed by nothing more than anecdotal evidence, and in this case, is a matter of state and local law, not federal law. The proposed amendment would create a new requirement for Certified Local Governments receiving funds through the Historic Preservation Fund, and would dictate to these local governments specific requirements about how they regulate their land use, even for projects with no federal assistance or involvement whatsoever. No evidence has been presented that this change is needed or will provide additional due process protections. In our view, it is highly inappropriate for Congress to engage in micromanaging local land use laws. We urge you not to pursue this proposed amendment.

These days more and more Americans are turning to the very heart of our common experience, to the institutions, history, and traditions that define us as a nation. It is our mission to ensure that these vital elements of our American heritage are preserved for generations to come. We appreciate the Subcommittee holding a hearing to examine the proposals outlined in the discussion draft, but urge you not to move forward with the Section 106 provisions in the discussion draft. As exemplified by the President's "Preserve America" Executive Order, it is a civic responsibility and a federal obligation to ensure that vital historic resources can be preserved for generations to come. The discussion draft proposals would take an extreme approach that no other Congress has taken in defining our federal preservation laws. Think of how ironic it would be—in the aftermath of September 11th when so many Americans have been focused on the icons of our national identity—to undermine the process that has preserved the World Trade Center site for posterity. We hope that you will reauthorize the laws that underpin historic preservation without undermining their integrity.

———

Mr. NUNES. Thank you, Ms. Wadhams. Ms. Matthews, you are recognized for 5 minutes.

STATEMENT OF JANET SNYDER MATTHEWS, ASSOCIATE DIRECTOR FOR CULTURAL RESOURCES, NATIONAL PARK SERVICE, WASHINGTON, D.C.

Ms. MATTHEWS. Thank you, Mr. Chairman. I am Jan Matthews, Associate Director, Cultural Resources, National Park Service, Department of Interior.

Thank you for this opportunity to provide an update on accomplishments of America's National Historic Preservation Program, authorized under the National Historic Preservation Act of 1966.

I formerly worked with Section 106 as State Historic Preservation Officer, appointed by then Florida Secretary of State Katherine Harris and Governor Jeb Bush.

We understand today that a bill to amend the National Act may be introduced based on a discussion draft recently provided to the Department of Interior. We respectfully request the Committee provide us with an opportunity to share our views should it be introduced prior to moving forward with a bill.

We also are interested in working with the Committee to resolve any unintended consequences resulting from implementation.

Our testimony today discusses concerns with the discussion draft provides background on nearly 40 years under the National Historic Preservation Act. Congress passed the Act in response to the recommendations of a special committee of the U.S. Conference of Mayors who urged establishment of a strong Federal preservation program to recognize and protect significant historic places in communities across the nation.

Communities were gravely concerned that the Federal Government routinely supported projects destroying their historic places without considering alternatives. The Conference of Mayors and the voting public who lobbied for the preservation passage of the Act knew then as we know better now that economic development and the health of communities depend on preserving the richness and variety of America's heritage.

One of the primary reasons the Act has been so successful is because it provides means of assuring that historic places are considered in the Federal planning process, while providing protections for property owners, privately owned.

Preserve America Executive Order 13287 signed by President Bush enjoins the Federal Government to provide leadership in protecting and celebrating historic assets for economic development and community revitalization. Heritage tourism depends on the preservation of historic places, one of the most important sources of revenue for many communities.

The proposed changes would limit the requirement that a Federal agency conduct a Section 106 review only to properties listed or determined eligible by the Secretary of Interior. Federal agencies would no longer be required to consider the potential impact on historic places currently identified as eligible to informal consultations between the state and Federal governments. Many private property owners rely upon this because many important historic properties have yet to be listed.

Federal agencies also use eligibility determinations to fulfill other mandates under other statutes, such as Federal Land Management Policy Act and NEPA, National Environmental Policy Act. Without a reliable source of information, without an efficient mechanism, other delays may result.

Changes in the Act that would compromise or eliminate identifying and considering historic places would jeopardize numerous historic resources because they would not be considered in the Federal planning process and the leadership and affirmative responsibility of Federal agencies under Section 110 and Section 106 and new mandates such as President Bush's new Preserve America initiative.

As the Nation evolves in diversity and complexity in every sector, we must ensure that the history of all Americans is identified, honored, and preserved. The law Congress passed in '66 is intentionally flexible to accommodate a changing nation's sense of what is historic and worthy of preservation. The Act created a remarkable national partnership network. Tribal and local governments played and decisive, in most ways co-equal public roles, in a system that has worked extraordinarily well for 40 years. The on-the-ground work of the program directly involves citizen input, delivered principally to our citizens through state, local, tribal governments—a demonstration of the success of our democracy because every partner, every citizen plays a role, has a voice in recognizing an preserving our heritages.

The authorization for this Historic Preservation Fund and the Advisory Council expires at the end of this fiscal year because of the success of the Fund and the important role of the Council to preserve heritage across the country. We look forward to working with the Committee to assure their continuation in the coming years.

Mr. Chairman, this concludes my prepared remarks. I would be pleased to answer any questions you or members may have.

[The prepared statement of Ms. Matthews follows:]

Statement of Janet Snyder Matthews, Associate Director for Cultural Resources, National Park Service, U.S. Department of the Interior

Mr. Chairman, thank you for the opportunity to provide an update on the accomplishments of America's national historic preservation program, authorized under the National Historic Preservation Act of 1966.

We understand that a bill to amend the National Historic Preservation Act (NHPA) may be introduced based on a discussion draft recently provided to the Department. We respectfully request that the Committee provide us an opportunity to share our views on the bill, should it be introduced, prior to moving forward with a bill. We also are interested in working with the Committee to resolve any unintended consequences resulting from the implementation of the NHPA. Our testimony today will discuss some of our concerns with the discussion draft and provide background on the nearly forty year history of the NHPA Program.

The NHPA establishes a collaborative approach to protect historic properties that embodies Secretary of the Interior Gale Norton's "Four Cs"—Communication, Consultation, and Cooperation, all in the service of Conservation. The NHPA creates partnerships among federal agencies, states, tribes, and local governments, which play a critical role in carrying out the key programs of the NHPA. These programs related to NHPA include the National Register of Historic Places, the section 106 consultation process, the Historic Preservation Fund, the Historic Preservation Tax Incentives Program, and Preserve America.

Governor-appointed State Historic Preservation Officers in 56 States and Territories assist citizens, units of local government, and public and private organizations to carry out their part of the national preservation program. State historic preservation programs locate, document, and assist citizens in nominating historic properties to the National Register, aid local governments and federal agencies in meeting historic preservation statutes, and assess the impact of federal projects on historic places. The work of state governments is essential to the preservation of our historic places.

Local governments also can play a formal role in the national preservation program by becoming Certified Local Governments. These important partners assist local citizens in inventorying historic buildings and neighborhoods, preserving and enhancing the historic values of these sites, working with local schools to ensure the next generation recognizes and values their local history, and coordinating with state governments to ensure the national historic preservation program meets local needs in the best manner possible.

Fifty-two tribal governments now have formally joined the national preservation program with established Tribal Preservation Officers. Tribal participation has enriched the national program by providing the Tribes' perspective on heritage, history, preservation, and sense of place.

Congress passed the NHPA of 1966 in response to the recommendations of a Special Committee on Historic Preservation of the U.S. Conference of Mayors. The conference urged that the United States establish a strong federal preservation program to support the recognition and protection of significant historic places in communities throughout the nation. Congress recognized in passing the NHPA that historical properties significant to the Nation's heritage were being lost or substantially altered at an increasing frequency.

As directed by Congress, the NHPA set in motion a process to reduce the loss of much of the nation's invaluable heritage and established the means for the federal government to provide leadership in the preservation of historic places in a unique partnership that remains highly effective today. The Conference of Mayors and others who lobbied for the passage of the Act knew then, as we know better now, that economic development and the health of communities are both dependent on preserving the richness and variety of America's heritage.

National Register of Historic Places

One of our most widely recognized national institutions is the National Register of Historic Places. In addition to recognizing national significance, the National Register recognizes "local historic significance" with two thirds (67%) of the properties listed in our National Register for their significance to local citizens and local history. The National Register now includes nearly 1.4 million properties in 79,000 listings nominated by citizens nationwide. There is hardly a city or town throughout the nation without a property listed in the National Register of Historic Places. Last fiscal year alone, 46,619 properties were listed in 1,537 nominations of historic places.

A Federal Preservation Officer, State Historic Preservation Officer, or Tribal Preservation Officer can nominate a property for listing in the National Register. During review of a proposed nomination, prior to being submitted to the Secretary, property owners and local officials are notified of the intent to nominate and public comment is solicited.

Owners of private property are given an opportunity to concur in or object to the nomination. If the owner of a private property, or the majority of private property owners for a property or district with multiple owners, objects to the nomination, the historic property cannot be listed in the National Register. In these instances, the property would be evaluated for a determination of eligibility. Less than 1 % of the nominations submitted to the Secretary are determinations of eligibility involving owner objections. Listing in the National Register or a determination of eligibility does not restrict a property owner from disposing of a historic property in any manner he or she sees fit. The private property owner is under no obligation to protect the historic property under federal law, and it can be torn down by its owner without federal government intervention.

The Section 106 Consultation Process

One of the primary reasons the NHPA has been so successful is because the consultation process under section 106 creates a means of assuring that historic properties are identified and considered in the federal planning process, including processes involved in the award of a federal grant or license. The section 106 consultation process requires a federal agency to determine if a proposed federal undertaking could affect historic properties. Historic properties include those listed in the National Register or those that are eligible for listing. If eligibility has not yet been determined, the federal agency can quickly and efficiently identify eligible properties through an informal consultation with the relevant state historic preservation offices or Tribal preservation offices. If questions arise about the eligibility of a given property, the more time-consuming process of a formal determination of eligibility may be sought.

The NHPA allows for flexibility for industries and agencies to comply with section 106 requirements while advancing and preserving the goal of protecting historic properties. The Advisory Council on Historic Preservation has the flexibility, under procedures which have undergone extensive public review, to develop administrative programmatic agreements tailored to the needs of specific federal programs. For example, this year the Federal Communications Commission implemented a nationwide programmatic agreement for the unique situation of constructing communication towers for wireless companies. It is this kind of flexibility allowed under the NHPA that has helped it adapt to new situations that have arisen over the past 39 years.

The Historic Preservation Fund

The NHPA also creates a national "cost-sharing" approach through the Historic Preservation Fund where the federal government provides a share of the financial resources needed to state, local and tribal governments, which, in turn, provide matching funds and share the benefits with citizens. The Historic Preservation Fund is a highly cost-effective cornerstone of the national preservation program with strong bipartisan support. It has been a model for state-legislated programs that provide grant monies based on programs designed under the NHPA. Certified Local Governments often use the 10% of the Historic Preservation Fund grants awarded to them for heritage tourism projects, which generates revenue for communities.

The Historic Preservation Tax Incentives Program

The Historic Preservation Tax Incentives Program, through the use of tax incentives, stimulates private-sector preservation and reuse of income-producing historic properties. Since its inception in 1976, the program has generated over $33 billion in historic preservation activity; in FY 2004 alone, a record-setting $3.88 billion in private investment was leveraged using federal historic preservation tax credits rehabilitating some 1,200 historic properties listed in the National Register and creating over 50,000 jobs and nearly 16,000 housing units.

The Advisory Council on Historic Preservation

The NHPA established the Advisory Council on Historic Preservation as the independent federal agency in the partnership dedicated to historic preservation and as the major policy advisor to federal agencies on historic preservation. The Council's members include representatives from every level of government and private citizens. It is the nation's advocate for full consideration of historic values in federal decision-making through its oversight of the section 106 process. The Council plays an essential role in reviewing federal programs and policies to further preservation efforts; providing training, guidance, and information to the public and federal entities; and recommending administrative and legislative improvements for protecting the nation's heritage.

Preserve America

The Department is working in partnership with the Council to further the goals of the new Preserve America Executive Order 13287 signed by President Bush. This Executive Order directs federal agencies to inventory and promote greater use of historical sites in partnership with state, tribal, and local governments. This initiative will provide more opportunities for preservation while increasing tourism and economic development by promoting historic and cultural preservation and encouraging greater public appreciation of our nation's treasures.

We would like to note some of our concerns with the discussion draft that was provided to the Department. The discussion draft proposes changes to NHPA that would limit the historical data collected through the National Register process. Under the proposed change, eligibility determinations would not continue to be made on properties where the owner objects to listing. In a related section, the discussion draft proposes to limit current section 106 review requirements to properties listed in the National Register or formally determined eligible by the Secretary of the Interior. It is unclear what this change could be interpreted to mean. This change could be interpreted to mean that federal agencies simply could not consider the potential impact of their projects on historic properties currently identified as eligible through informal consultations between the state and federal governments. This interpretation would narrow the consideration of historic properties in the planning of federal projects and could place historic resources at risk. The discussion draft also could be interpreted to continue to require eligibility determinations, but through the imposition of a formal process through the Secretary of the Interior. This interpretation could place a tremendous administrative burden on the Department of the Interior and would result in a delay of federal projects. Most historic properties, including the Golden Gate Bridge and the Mission San Juan Capistrano in California, were neither listed on the National Register nor formally determined eligible by the Secretary at the time of a proposed federal undertaking. They were evaluated as eligible on the basis of informal consultation during the planning stage. Many important historic properties have yet to be listed.

The NHPA today acknowledges that finding and evaluating our historic places is ongoing. It is a process that requires federal agencies to develop enough information on federal projects to avoid needless destruction of those historic places. Many private property owners benefit from the current review process. Restricting the development of that information will inevitably lead to a cumbersome review process and destruction of important resources, including those that could enhance the value of private property, and that could easily have been avoided.

Last year, state historic preservation programs were asked by federal agencies to review approximately 104,172 federal projects. They found that in the vast majority (88,212) of these projects, no historic properties were identified or the proposed project was determined to have no effect on historic properties. As part of the informal consultation, states and federal agencies concurred that some 22,700 properties not previously recognized were, in their judgment, eligible for the National Register, and therefore should be considered in the federal planning process under section 106 of the NHPA. Under the discussion draft, those 22,700 properties would be eliminated from consideration during the federal planning process or would have had to undergo potentially lengthy formal eligibility determinations. Compared with the 22,700 properties determined eligible through informal consultations, only nineteen properties were formally determined eligible for the National Register by the Secretary as a part of the section 106 process.

Federal agencies can satisfy section 106 quickly and efficiently by working directly with state historic preservation offices to identify eligible properties and consider them in the federal planning process. Federal agencies currently use informal eligibility determinations under section 106 to fulfill other mandates required under other statutes, such as the Federal Land Management Policy Act (FLPMA). Without a reliable source of information on historic properties, additional processes and evaluations may need to be developed in order to meet the statutory requirements. Delays can occur in a wide variety of determinations made by the Secretary under FLPMA, including those related to minerals development.

State, local, and tribal governments have enacted laws that establish additional protections and, in some cases, financial incentives for listed or eligible properties beyond their consideration in the federal planning process under federal law. A number of states have passed statutes that require consideration of historic places in the planning of state projects similar to the requirement in section 106 of the NHPA, and that provide grants and tax incentives. More than 2,500 communities have local laws establishing historic preservation commissions, and nearly 1,500 of those communities have applied for and become Certified Local Governments under the NHPA.

Because history does not stop, the nation's understanding of what is worthy of preservation changes with the passage of time and the growing appreciation of the breadth and depth of our nation's heritage. The law passed in 1966 provides the flexibility needed to accommodate a nation's changing sense of what is historic and worthy of preservation. The NHPA has created a remarkable national partnership network, one in which state, tribal, and local governments play decisive and, in most ways, co-equal public roles to the federal government in a system that has worked well for nearly 40 years. The federal government, acting through the National Park Service, sets professional and performance standards, provides technical assistance, advice, and training, and provides oversight and approval roles. But the on-the-ground work of the national preservation program directly involves citizen input and is delivered principally to our citizens through state, local, and tribal governments.

The authorization for the Historic Preservation Fund and the Advisory Council on Historic Preservation expires at the end of Fiscal Year 2005. Because of the success of the fund and the important role that the Advisory Council plays as a partner in our efforts to preserve historic places across the country, we look forward to working with the Committee to assure the continuation of this partnership in the coming years.

Mr. Chairman, this concludes my prepared remarks. I would be pleased to answer any questions you or members of the committee may have.

Mr. NUNES. Thank you, Ms. Matthews. Mr. Nau, you are recognized for 5 minutes.

STATEMENT OF JOHN NAU, CHAIRMAN, ADVISORY COUNCIL ON HISTORIC PRESERVATION, WASHINGTON, D.C.

Mr. NAU. Mr. Chairman, it is with a great deal of pleasure that I come before you today to talk about the reauthorization of the Advisory Council on Historic Preservation.

I am John Nau, Chairman of the Advisory Council. We look forward to working closely with this Committee to craft this important legislation, and I personally appreciate the speed with which the Committee has taken up this legislation.

Last year, then Chairman Radanovich introduced H.R. 3223, which contained many of the provisions of the current discussion draft. In addition to the ACHP reauthorization, membership changes, and other technical changes that were included in H.R. 3223, the discussion draft includes reauthorization of Historic Preservation Fund, an important additional element supported by us.

Last year, during the hearings lead up to H.R. 3223, an anomaly of the current National Historic Preservation Act became very evident. Certain local jurisdictions linked their historic preservation ordinances to the eligibility of property for listing on the National Register of Historic Places, imposing limitation on future use of the property through exercise of local rather than Federal law.

In order to address this, we held discussions with the Committee staff concerning elimination of the requirement that the Secretary make a formal determination of eligibility when a nomination is submitted over property owner's objection.

Changes to the law that preserve a property owner's rights when he or she perceives no benefit to eligibility just simply makes sense to me.

Along that same line, we discussed including a halt to any further processing of a nomination in the face of a property owner's objection. While we think that there is an opportunity to codify our understanding of this concern, the language in the discussion draft appears to go further than simply National Register nominations and may impact the Section 106 process governing the planning of Federal projects. And that is very different case.

We would like to see this additional language removed or modified in any final legislation.

Section 106 of the National Historic Preservation Act requires Federal agencies make a reasonable and good faith effort to identify historic properties listed or eligible for listing on the National Register. Through the process when Federal activities are initiated, project managers determine what historic resources are present and may be impacted by that action. Were a static, final, or complete listing of potentially eligible properties feasible, this obligation could be met simply by consulting a list.

However, as you have heard, history continues to be made and additional properties become eligible for National Register recognition daily.

So even if the resources were available to make such a list, a static listing is simply not feasible.

Again, a recent example that you have heard numerous times here is the World Trade Center Ground Zero. Were it not for the current formulation of the eligibility determination process in

Section 106, absolutely no consideration would have been given to this nationally important site.

You have also heard of two classes of historic resources that would have virtually no protection without the 106 process. Archaeological sites and Native American and Native Hawaiian religious and cultural sites. Very few are listed or determined eligible at this time, and, therefore, they would not be taken into consideration where the language of the proposed section—as Section 4, as proposed in the discussion draft be adapted.

The ACHP has many tools to modify the Section 106 process to ensure that its goals are reasonably met. As an example, we recently entered into a programmatic agreement with the FCC regarding cell tower construction. We exempted gas pipelines as well as exempting the interstate highway system. We streamlined the review process for over 30,000 units of cold war era military housing—administrative and regulatory solutions rather than a blanket legislative exclusion have served the Nation and this Congress well.

Mr. Chairman, we look forward to working with the Committee toward developing final language that will make the necessary changes to the NHPAA, reauthorizing the ACHP, as well as the National Historic Fund, and codify important property rights language that protects the legitimate interests of property owners in the National Register nomination process.

However, we believe that the ACHP is currently well equipped to address any concerns about the scope of the 106 process, and do not believe hat changes to the statute are necessary.

Again, thank you very much for the opportunity to present our position before the Committee.

[The prepared statement of Mr. Nau follows:]

Statement of John L. Nau, III, Chairman, Advisory Council on Historic Preservation

My name is John L. Nau, III, and I am pleased to submit my testimony on behalf of the Advisory Council on Historic Preservation (ACHP). At the outset, let me note the ACHP's appreciation for the continued interest and support that the Committee has demonstrated for the ACHP and the Federal historic preservation program. We view our relationship with the Committee as an essential ingredient of developing and implementing an effective national historic preservation program. We look forward to working closely with you on the future development of this important legislation.

I would also like to express my pleasure with the speed with which the Committee has addressed the important issue of reauthorization of the ACHP and the Historic Preservation Fund. We are gratified that the Committee is taking up these issues early in the session and we are eager to assist you in bringing this legislative initiative to fruition. There are elements of the legislation, embodied in the discussion draft bill, that are crucial to the effective functioning of the national historic preservation program and we join with the Administration and our preservation partners to urge their early enactment.

By way of background, let me state for the record that the ACHP sought reauthorization legislation in the previous Congress, and the necessary provisions, along with a short list of operational improvements, was introduced by former Chairman Radanovich as H.R. 3223. This Committee held a hearing June 3, 2003, and I had the pleasure of testifying. With the Committee's permission, I would like to submit my written statement from that hearing for the record, as it provides detailed information about the ACHP, its need for reauthorization, and the provisions of last session's bill, which are largely incorporated into the current discussion draft.

We were disappointed that H.R. 3223 was not enacted in the 108th Congress, but we look at it as the benchmark for legislation now being considered. During development of H.R. 3223, the Committee brought to our attention several concerns with the operation of the historic preservation program and we endeavored to work cooperatively to address the Committee's concerns. We intend that this spirit shared by the ACHP and the Committee that produced H.R. 3223 will continue as we move forward.

As the President's appointee to lead the principal Federal agency charged with advising the President and the Congress on historic preservation matters, I find much to support in the bill. However, the inclusion of certain provisions, as drafted, seems to challenge some of the fundamental principles embodied in the National Historic Preservation Act (NHPA). Since its enactment in 1966, the NHPA has served preservation and our Nation well.

Let me start by summarizing those provisions that are needed and desirable improvements in the NHPA. First, the discussion draft would extend the authorization for $150 million annually from the proceeds of oil and gas leases on the Outer Continental Shelf to be made available for the Historic Preservation Fund. We believe this concept of using part of the proceeds from the depletion of the Nation's non-renewable resources to preserve and enhance another non-renewable resource, our cultural heritage, is sound and merits continuation. The Fund supports the valuable activities of the various State Historic Preservation Officers and Tribal Historic Preservation Officers, our principal partners in carrying out the NHPA's authorities. In addition, the Fund makes possible the President's proposed Preserve America grants program. Extending this authority through FY 2012 is essential and is welcomed by the ACHP.

Second, we strongly support the provisions of H.R. 3223 that have been incorporated into the discussion draft. Amendments that expand the membership of the ACHP, provide the ACHP with flexibility in the provision of administrative services and its donations account, and offer it new opportunities to cooperate with Federal agencies to help them advance historic preservation goals through their assistance programs, along with some necessary technical amendments, are all positive features and are supported by the ACHP. We thank you for their inclusion.

We welcome the Committee's attention to a key need of the ACHP, the extension of its appropriations authority. As requested by the Administration and embodied in H.R. 3223, the NHPA would be amended to provide the ACHP with a permanent appropriations authority. This would recognize the ACHP's important, permanent program responsibilities within the administrative structure created by the NHPA and place the ACHP on an even footing with its sister Federal agencies.

The discussion draft before us today has reverted to a time limited and capped appropriation authorization. We believe that this approach to authorization is contrary to the central role that the ACHP plays in the national historic preservation program, which is a permanent assignment that does not diminish over time. The ACHP is rare among Federal agencies in having a statutory charge to advise and report to both the President and the Congress, thus providing the ACHP with a special ongoing interaction with the Congress and this Committee. We believe that this close working relationship diminishes the need for a periodic formal legislative reauthorization process.

Furthermore, the amounts specified in the proposed annual authorization are below our FY 2005 appropriation and the President's FY 2006 request. The authorization ceilings in the discussion draft for FY 2007 through FY 2012 also are below what we anticipate will be the President's requests, simply based on the routine escalation of the costs of doing business at current levels. It was this exact problem that brought us to the 108th Congress seeking an appropriations authorization two years before our existing authorization expired.

I would now like to turn to two new provisions in the discussion draft that were not included in H.R. 3223. These are found in Sections 2, 3, and 4 of the discussion draft. Sections 2 and 3 address a concern that was raised in the 2003 hearings before this Committee with regard to the protection of the rights of property owners in the nomination process for the National Register of Historic Places. Without recounting the details of the case brought to the Committee's attention, the essence of the issue was that the NHPA currently provides the opportunity for a property owner to object to the listing of his or her property on the National Register of Historic Places.

The National Register was created by the Congress in 1966 to provide a comprehensive listing of properties significant in the Nation's history, architecture, archeology, culture, and engineering, at the national, State, and local level. This listing was to be used as a guide to the historic properties that warranted Federal financial assistance and consideration in the Federal project planning process. However, the intended comprehensive list has not been completed, due to the limited resources available to State Historic Preservation Officers for this task.

In 1980, responding to certain negative tax implications from National Register listing, Congress introduced a provision allowing an owner to object to formal listing, thereby avoiding the detrimental economic consequences imposed by the Internal Revenue Code should the property be redeveloped. The amended NHPA barred listing in the National Register over an owner's objection, but directed the Secretary of the Interior to make a formal determination of eligibility for the National Register in the case of any property nomination submitted to the Secretary over an owner's objection.

Over the past quarter century, much has changed. The negative tax consequences of National Register listing have been abolished and accordingly listing no longer impacts a property owner's rights through the workings of Federal preservation law. Unfortunately, outside of the sphere of Federal law and policy, certain local laws, although rare, have used the Federal designation process as the basis for the application of stringent local preservation restrictions. This has presented the issue of "linkage," i.e., a local regulatory consequence that flows from the Federal National Register nomination process regardless of a property owner's objection to the nomination. This was the situation that brought the case of a Los Angeles property owner to the Committee's attention at its 2003 hearing.

While the ACHP sees this situation as rare, nevertheless we worked with the Committee staff, in the form of a drafting service and in fulfillment of our NHPA charge to advise both the executive and legislative branches on preservation matters, to prepare an appropriate legislative solution. Those discussions resulted in three potential amendments to the NHPA. First, the current requirement that the Secretary make a formal determination of a property's eligibility for the National Register when a nomination was submitted over an owner's objection would be stricken. This seemed reasonable, in that the owner had expressed disapproval of formal designation by raising the objection. Continued processing, even for the less formal eligibility determination, seemed on its face at odds with respecting the owner's stated objection. With regard to the unintended linkage to local law that seriously impeded the use of the Los Angeles property in ways that were not intended by the NHPA, the change appeared to address the problem in large part. This provision is found in the first part of Section 2(a) of the discussion draft.

Closely related to this was the idea that, if an owner lodges an objection as provided for in the NHPA, the nomination process should not be allowed to move forward. In the Los Angeles case, the subsequent processing of the nomination, despite the property owner's objection, gave rise to a local decision to impose the local landmark restrictions. This outcome was clearly contrary to the intent of the Congress when it amended the NHPA in 1980. As a result, our discussions with Committee staff led to the development of a provision that the owner's objection would halt any further processing of the nomination process. The current version of that provision is found in the second part of Section 2(a) of the discussion draft.

The provisions that the ACHP assisted in developing have been altered in the discussion draft. While the first component is essentially the same, the discussion draft introduces a new phrase that goes beyond our discussions and causes us concern. That is the addition of the language "including making any determination regarding the eligibility of the property or district for such inclusion or designation." While the intent of this language is unclear, we are concerned that it may extend the owner objection provision beyond the confines of the formal National Register nomination procedure and impact the process used in the Federal project planning process mandated by Section 106 of the NHPA. We recommend to the Committee that this additional language be removed. The previously outlined provisions provide a significant and sufficient protection for property owners.

Our principal concern with the discussion draft is found in Section 4. That section proposes a significant change in the current scope of the fundamental Federal protection for historic properties that the Congress enacted in 1966 and expanded in 1976. As currently written, Section 106 of the NHPA requires Federal agencies to take into account the effect of their undertakings on properties listed or eligible for listing in the National Register of Historic Places. In its wisdom, the Congress recognized in 1976, ten years after the passage of the original NHPA and the creation of the National Register, that the National Register was a work in progress and would remain so for many years to come. As noted above, it was simply not possible to complete statewide surveys of historic properties with the amount of resources being made available. Likewise, the passage of time inevitably leads to additional properties meeting the criteria for listing in the National Register. Taking a page from President Nixon's Executive Order 11593 of 1971, the Congress amended Section 106 to require Federal agencies to consider eligible as well as formally listed properties in the Federal historic preservation review process.

Since 1976, this expanded Section 106 process has served both the Federal Government and the Nation's cultural patrimony well. Implemented by rules issued by the ACHP, the process requires Federal agencies to make a reasonable and good faith effort to identify historic properties that are listed or may meet the criteria for listing in the National Register when they may be impacted by a Federal action. The involved Federal agencies determine what historic resources are present and may be impacted by their actions. The process has become well integrated into Federal project planning and results in even-handed consideration of historic property impacts as an integral part of environmental assessment and decision-making.

Section 4 of the discussion draft would fundamentally alter this established process. It would limit the Federal agency obligation to consider only those properties that had been previously formally listed in the National Register or formally determined eligible for the National Register by the Secretary of the Interior. I must emphasize for the Committee that most historic properties that are actually eligible for the National Register have not gone through the formal nomination and designation process. Likewise, few have been formally determined eligible for the National Register by the Secretary for the simple reason that essentially the only route to such a determination is through the previously described process of a nomination moving forward to the Secretary when an owner objects. These cases are few and far between.

The routine eligibility determination for Section 106 purposes is made by consensus between the State Historic Preservation Officer and the Federal agency with a limited degree of formality and paperwork. By practice, these "consensus" determinations of eligibility efficiently provide the agency with the basic information it needs to factor historic preservation impacts into planning. Section 106 does not provide a listed or eligible property with absolute protection from harm; far from it, the process simply requires the Federal agency to consider the potential impacts and assess options to minimize that harm.

The proposed amendment would eliminate the current obligation of Federal agencies to take affirmative steps to identify properties not yet formally recognized as historic but that might be impacted by a Federal project. Lest one infer that such properties are of minor or marginal significance, let me note but a few of the historic properties that have been brought into Section 106 review through the current eligibility system: the World Trade Center Site, and Saarinen's TWA Terminal, in New York City; the historic Del Monte Hotel in Monterey, California; the Chancellorsville Historic District adjacent to Chancellorsville National Battlefield Park, Virginia; Murphy Farm, a site significant in the history of the NAACP located next to Harpers Ferry National Historical Park, West Virginia; and the building where the first atomic bomb was assembled at Los Alamos, New Mexico. In each of these cases, important historic properties were saved through consideration in the Section 106 process, which could not have happened if the proposed amendment to Section 106 had been law.

I particularly want to draw the Committee's attention to two classes of historic resources that would virtually fall off the Section 106 review table if Section 4 were enacted. First, by their nature, archeological sites are rarely known until Federal project-driven surveys uncover them. The devastation to that heritage would be dramatic. Many such sites are associated with Native American heritage; other important sites include the colonial-era African Burial Ground in New York City and the Kanaka Village Site at the Hudson Bay Company's Fort Vancouver in Oregon. But for the current determination of eligibility process, these sites would have been destroyed without any consideration by Federal project planners.

Second, in 1990, Congress made it clear that the National Register and the protections of Section 106 extend to historic properties of traditional religious and cultural significance to Native Americans and Native Hawaiians. Regrettably, through no fault of Indian tribes and Native Hawaiian organizations, the National Register currently contains but a small sampling of the sites that these parties hold as sacred elements of their cultural heritage. Enactment of Section 4 would strip Indian tribes and Native Hawaiian organizations of any effective use of Section 106 to protect their irreplaceable heritage. On that ground alone, I would strongly oppose the suggested amendment to Section 106.

It is important to bring to the Committee's attention that the existing Section 106 regulations provide useful tools to flex and modify the Section 106 process to ensure that its goals are reasonably met. The ACHP can point proudly to its use of the these tools in just the past three years to adjust and streamline the process to adapt Section 106 to new challenges and contemporary needs.

- We have used the authority to exempt Federal activities affecting certain kinds of resources to deal with historic interstate pipelines, such as the famous "Big Inch" and "Little Inch" pipelines that contributed to the winning of World War

II, and the management of the Interstate Highway System, which must be recognized as the most significant public works project of the 20th century and has shaped our lives today. Through these exemptions, the historic importance of these properties has been recognized without imposing the formal requirements of Section 106 reviews.
- We have issued simplified program comments to deal with nearly 30,000 units of Cold War-era military housing that warrant consideration as historically significant, thereby eliminating thousands of potential individual Section 106 reviews.
- We have recently adopted a programmatic agreement that streamlines and simplifies the process for considering the impact of federally licensed wireless communication towers in a way that introduces certainty and finality to the Federal Communications Commission's regulation of cell tower construction.

These administrative solutions were developed in cooperation with Federal agencies and demonstrate the ACHP's commitment to use the tools found in existing law to provide practical answers to problems they encounter in the Section 106 process. In doing so, we improve program efficiency while honoring the fundamental principles of the NHPA. I strongly believe that these kinds of administrative and regulatory solutions, rather than legislative alteration of the important protections of Section 106, can resolve any concerns that the discussion draft seeks to address.

In sum, the discussion draft contains important amendments to the NHPA that need enactment. We applaud and support those provision that will continue and strengthen the role of the ACHP and the Historic Preservation Fund, with the substitution of the language in H.R. 3223 as it pertains to the ACHP authorization. However, the ACHP opposes legislative alteration of Section 106 as proposed in the discussion draft. Our established administrative processes, with a recent and demonstrated track record, can address changing needs, and we are committed to use them to solve emerging problems. We hope the Committee will endorse the current system, which has been carefully tuned and refined over the years, and refrain from embarking on a path of unnecessary alteration of the NHPA.

We welcome the opportunity to work with the Committee to examine ways that we can refine and strengthen our capacity to address its concerns.

[The statement submitted for the record by Mr. Nau follows:]

Testimony for the record submitted by John L. Nau, III, Chairman, Advisory Council on Historic Preservation to the Subcommittee on National Parks, Recreation, and Public Lands, The Honorable George Radanovich, Chairman

OVERSIGHT HEARING ON REAUTHORIZATION OF THE ADVISORY COUNCIL ON HISTORIC PRESERVATION AND THE NATIONAL HISTORIC PRESERVATION ACT

JUNE 3, 2003

SUMMARY STATEMENT

An independent Federal agency, the Advisory Council on Historic Preservation (ACHP) promotes historic preservation nationally by providing a forum for influencing Federal activities, programs, and policies that impact historic properties. In furtherance of this objective, the ACHP seeks reauthorization of its appropriations in accordance with the provisions of the National Historic Preservation Act of 1966, as amended (16 U.S.C. 470 et seq.) (NHPA).

The ACHP offers amendments to its authorities that we believe will strengthen our ability to meet our responsibilities under NHPA, and to provide leadership and coordination in the Federal historic preservation program. As part of that responsibility, and as requested by the Subcommittee, the ACHP also provides its views on the adequacy of protections for private property owners in the process of evaluating properties for inclusion in the National Register of Historic Places.

BACKGROUND

The ACHP was established by Title II of the NHPA. NHPA charges the ACHP with advising the President and the Congress on historic preservation matters and entrusts the ACHP with the unique mission of advancing historic preservation within the Federal Government and the National Historic Preservation Program. In FY 2002, the ACHP adopted the following mission statement:

The Advisory Council on Historic Preservation promotes the preservation, enhancement, and productive use of our Nation's historic resources, and advises the President and Congress on national historic preservation policy.

The ACHP's authority and responsibilities are principally derived from NHPA. General duties of the ACHP are detailed in Section 202 (16 U.S.C. 470j) and include:

- advising the President and Congress on matters relating to historic preservation;
- encouraging public interest and participation in historic preservation;
- recommending policy and tax studies as they affect historic preservation;
- advising State and local governments on historic preservation legislation;
- encouraging training and education in historic preservation;
- reviewing Federal policies and programs and recommending improvements; and
- informing and educating others about the ACHP's activities.

Under Section 106 of NHPA (16 U.S.C. 470f), the ACHP reviews Federal actions affecting historic properties to ensure that historic preservation needs are considered and balanced with Federal project requirements. It achieves this balance through the "Section 106 review process," which applies whenever a Federal action has the potential to impact historic properties. As administered by the ACHP, the process guarantees that State and local governments, Indian tribes, businesses and organizations, and private citizens will have an effective opportunity to participate in Federal project planning when historic properties they value may be affected.

Under Section 211 of NHPA (16 U.S.C. 470s) the ACHP is granted rulemaking authority for Section 106. The ACHP also has consultative and other responsibilities under Sections 101, 110, 111, 203, and 214 of NHPA, and in accordance with the National Environmental Policy Act (42 U.S.C. 4321 et seq.) is considered an agency with "special expertise" to comment on environmental impacts involving historic properties and other cultural resources.

The ACHP plays a pivotal role in the National Historic Preservation Program. Founded as a unique partnership among Federal, State, and local governments, Indian tribes, and the public to advance the preservation of America's heritage while recognizing contemporary needs, the partnership has matured and expanded over time. The Secretary of the Interior and the ACHP have distinct but complementary responsibilities for managing the National Historic Preservation Program. The Secretary, acting through the Director of the National Park Service, maintains the national inventory of historic properties, sets standards for historic preservation, administers financial assistance and programs for tribal, State, and local participation, and provides technical preservation assistance.

The ACHP also plays a key role in shaping historic preservation policy and programs at the highest levels of the Administration. It coordinates the national program, assisting Federal agencies in meeting their preservation responsibilities. Through its administration of Section 106, the ACHP works with Federal agencies, States, tribes, local governments, applicants for Federal assistance, and other affected parties to ensure that their interests are considered in the process. It helps parties reach agreement on measures to avoid or resolve conflicts that may arise between development needs and preservation objectives, including mitigation of harmful impacts.

The ACHP is uniquely suited to its task. As an independent agency, it brings together through its membership Federal agency heads, representatives of State and local governments, historic preservation leaders and experts, Native American representatives, and private citizens to shape national policies and programs dealing with historic preservation. The ACHP's diverse membership is reflected in its efforts to seek sensible, cost-effective ways to mesh preservation goals with other public needs. Unlike other Federal agencies or private preservation organizations, the ACHP incorporates a variety of interests and viewpoints in fulfilling its statutory duties, broadly reflecting the public interest. Recommended solutions are reached that reflect both the impacts on irreplaceable historic properties and the needs of today's society.

New Directions. Since assuming the Chairmanship in November 2001, I have tried to ensure that the ACHP takes the leadership role envisioned for it in NHPA. NHPA established a national policy to "foster conditions under which our modern society and our prehistoric and historic resources can exist in productive harmony and fulfill the social, economic and other requirements of present and future generations." Among other things, the statute directed Federal agencies to foster conditions that help attain the national goal of historic preservation; to act as faithful stewards of federally owned, administered, or controlled historic resources for present and future generations; and to offer maximum encouragement and assistance to other public and private preservation efforts through a variety of means.

In creating the ACHP, Congress recognized the value of having an independent entity to provide advice, coordination, and oversight of NHPA's implementation by Federal agencies. The ACHP remains the only Federal entity created solely to

45

address historic preservation issues, and helps to bridge differences in this area among Federal agencies, and between the Federal Government and States, Indian tribes, local governments, and citizens. While the administration of the historic preservation review process established by Section 106 of NHPA is very important and a significant ACHP responsibility, we believe that the ACHP's mission is broader than simply managing that process.

With the new direction, the ACHP members are committed to promoting the preservation and appreciation of historic properties across the Nation by undertaking new initiatives that include:

- developing an Executive order (Executive Order 13287, "Preserve America," signed by the President March 3, 2003) to promote the benefits of preservation, to improve Federal stewardship of historic properties, and to foster recognition of such properties as national assets to be used for economic, educational, and other purposes;
- creating an initiative for the White House ("Preserve America," announced by First Lady Laura Bush March 3, 2003) to stimulate creative partnerships among all levels of government and the private sector to preserve and actively use historic resources to stimulate a better appreciation of America's history and diversity;
- using Council meetings to learn from local government and citizens how the Federal Government can effectively participate in local heritage tourism initiatives and promote these strategies to Federal agencies and tourism professionals;
- effectively communicating its mission and activities to its stakeholders as well as the general public;
- pursuing partnerships with Federal agencies to streamline and increase the effectiveness of the Federal historic preservation review process; and
- improving the Native American program, which the ACHP has identified as a critical element in the implementation of an effective Federal historic preservation program and review process.

The ACHP's 20 statutorily designated members address policy issues, direct program initiatives, and make recommendations regarding historic preservation to the President, Congress, and heads of other Federal agencies. The Council members meet four times per year to conduct business, holding two meetings in Washington, D.C., and two in other communities where relevant preservation issues can be explored.

In 2002 we reorganized the ACHP membership and staff to expand the members' role and to enhance work efficiencies as well as member-staff interaction. To best use the talents and energy of the 20 Council members and ensure that they fully participate in advancing the ACHP's goals and programs, three member program committees were created: Federal Agency Programs; Preservation Initiatives; and Communications, Education, and Outreach.

In addition, we created an Executive Committee comprised of myself and the vice chairman of the ACHP and the chairman of each of the other committees to assist in the governance of the ACHP. Several times a year, we appoint panels of members to formulate comments on Section 106 cases. Member task forces and committees are also formed to pursue specific tasks, such as policy development or regulatory reform oversight. On average, three such subgroups are at work at any given time during the year. Each meets about five to six times in the course of its existence, is served by one to three staff members, and produces reports, comments, and policy recommendations.

The staff carries out the day-to-day work of the ACHP and provides all support services for Council members. To reflect and support the work of the committees, the Executive Director reorganized the ACHP staff into three program offices to mirror the committee structure. Staff components are under the supervision of the Executive Director, who is based in the Washington, D.C., office; there is also a small field office in Lakewood, Colorado.

PROPOSED AMENDMENTS TO THE NATIONAL HISTORIC PRESERVATION ACT

Background to Reauthorization. The ACHP has traditionally had its appropriations authorized on a multi-year cycle in Title II of NHPA (Section 212, 16 U.S.C. 470t). The current cycle runs through FY 2005 and authorizes $4 million annually. These funds are provided to support the programs and operations of the ACHP. Title II of NHPA also sets forth the general authorities and structure of the ACHP.

For FY 2004, the President's budget seeks $4.1 million for the ACHP. Because this is over the authorization limit, the Executive Office of the President directed the ACHP to propose any legislation required to modify its authorization to be consistent with the President's Budget. The ACHP is therefore seeking amendments to the authorizing legislation at this time. At its February and May 2003 meetings, the ACHP endorsed an approach to the reauthorization issue. The approach addresses the immediate appropriations authority issue and also seeks amendments to the ACHP's composition and authorities to better enable the ACHP to achieve its mission goals. The changes proposed by the ACHP are explained in this overview; specific statutory language will be provided to the Subcommittee at a later date.

Appropriations Authorization. This section would amend the current time-limited authorization and replace it with a permanent appropriations authorization. When the ACHP was created in 1966, its functions were exclusively advisory and limited and the agency was lodged administratively in the Department of the Interior. Since then, the Congress has amended the NHPA to establish the ACHP as an independent Federal agency and give it a range of program authorities crucial to the success of the National Historic Preservation Program.

Not unlike the Commission of Fine Arts (CFA) and the National Capital Planning Commission (NCPC), the ACHP now functions as a small but important Federal agency, carrying out both advisory and substantive program duties. Specific language creating a permanent appropriations authorization would draw upon the similar statutory authorities of the CFA and NCPC. No ceiling to the annual appropriations authorization would be included in the authorizing legislation, but rather the appropriate funding limits would be established through the annual appropriations process.

Expansion of Membership. This section would expand the membership of the ACHP by directing the President to designate the heads of three additional Federal agencies as members of the ACHP. The ACHP has been aggressively pursuing partnerships with Federal agencies in recent years and has found the results to be greatly beneficial to meeting both Federal agency historic preservation responsibilities and the ACHP's own mission goals. Experience has shown that these partnerships are fostered and enhanced by having the agency participate as a full-fledged member of the ACHP, giving it both a voice and a stake in the ACHP's actions. The amendment would bring the total number of Federal ACHP members to nine and expand the ACHP membership to 23, an administratively manageable number that preserves the current majority of non-Federal members. A technical amendment to adjust quorum requirements would also be included.

Authority and Direction to Improve Coordination with Federal Funding Agencies. This section would give the ACHP the authority and direction to work cooperatively with Federal funding agencies to assist them in determining appropriate uses of their existing grants programs for advancing the purposes of NHPA. For example, it is our experience that programs such as the Historic Preservation Fund (HPF) administered through the States by the Department of the Interior have the flexibility to provide matching seed money to a local non-profit organization to support a heritage tourism program.

The ACHP would work with agencies and grant recipients to examine the effectiveness of existing grant programs, evaluate the adequacy of funding levels, and help the agencies determine whether changes in the programs would better meet preservation and other needs. Any recommendations would be developed in close cooperation with the Federal funding agencies themselves, many of whom sit as ACHP members, and with the States. The proposed amendment would also allow the ACHP to work cooperatively with Federal funding agencies in the administration of their grant programs.

Technical Amendments. This section would provide four technical changes that would improve ACHP operations:

1. Authorize the Governor, who is a presidentially appointed member of the ACHP, to designate a voting representative to participate in the ACHP activities in the Governor's absence. Currently this authority is extended to Federal agencies and other organizational members. The amendment would recognize that the personal participation of a Governor cannot always be assumed, much like that of a Cabinet secretary.
2. Authorize the ACHP to engage administrative support services from sources other than the Department of the Interior. The current law requires the ACHP's administrative services to be provided by the Department of the Interior on a reimbursable basis. The amendment would authorize the ACHP to obtain any or all of those services from other Federal agencies or the private sector. The amendment would further the goals of the FAIR Act and improve ACHP efficiency by allowing the ACHP to obtain necessary services on the most beneficial terms.

3. Clarify that the ACHP's donation authority (16 U.S.C. 470m(g)) includes the ability of the ACHP to actively solicit such donations.
4. Adjust the quorum requirements to accommodate expanded ACHP membership.

VIEWS ON THE ADEQUACY OF PRIVATE PROPERTY PROTECTIONS IN THE NATIONAL REGISTER PROCESS

The Committee has requested our views on the adequacy of protections for private property owners during the process for evaluating and registering properties for inclusion in the National Register of Historic Places.

The National Register is the keystone of the National Historic Preservation Program. Through the professional application of objective criteria, a comprehensive listing of what is truly important in American history has been systematically compiled. The ACHP has direct experience with the National Register review and evaluation process through its administration of Section 106 of NHPA. As part of planning, unless properties are already listed in the National Register of Historic Places, determinations of eligibility for inclusion in the National Register must be made when such properties may be impacted by Federal or federally assisted actions.

We are unaware of problems with the protection of the rights of private property owners in the Section 106 process, since the determination is made for planning purposes only and for consideration by Federal agencies in taking into account the effects of their actions.

We do believe it is important to distinguish between actual listing in the National Register, which may result in tax and other benefits and legally must include opportunities for property owners to object to such listing, and determinations of eligibility which are used for Federal planning. It is our understanding that in rare instances, some States' legislation and some local ordinances include "eligibility for inclusion in the National Register" to trigger the State or local review process. It is our opinion that determinations of eligibility should not by themselves automatically trigger or link to a State or local review process without due process and additional protections of private property owners' rights. It is also our understanding that State Historic Preservation Offices, such as Texas, are generally discouraging eligibility from being included in State laws and local ordinances to ensure adequate private property protections.

States have varying approaches to dealing with the overall issue of notification and objection. Public notices, hearings, and other mechanisms are used when large historic districts are being considered. In the case of smaller districts or individual properties, written notification is provided. In Texas, notifications are sent out to the property owner, the county judge, the chief elected official, and the local preservation board chair of pending listings in the National Register with an opportunity for making their views known. In New York, if an objection to a nomination is received from an owner, that nomination does not proceed. An official representative from the New York State Historic Preservation Office will speak with the property owner and explain the effects of listing in the National Register. In many instances, owners will withdraw their objections once they understand the implication of such listing.

In summary, we think that as a function of Federal law and Federal administrative practice there are generally adequate protections for the rights of private property owners in the National Register process.

CONCLUSION

The ACHP has reached a level of maturity as an independent Federal agency and as a key partner in the National Historic Preservation Program to warrant continued support from the Congress. We believe that reauthorization, coupled with periodic oversight by this Subcommittee and the annual review provided by the Appropriations Committees, is fully justified by our record of accomplishment. We hope that the Subcommittee will favorably consider this request, including our recommended technical amendments.

We appreciate the Subcommittee's interest in these issues, and thank you for your consideration and the opportunity to present our views.

––––––––

Mr. NUNES. Thank you, Mr. Nau. Thank you for your testimony, and thank all of you for being here once again.

The reason that we put out this draft is so that we can have discussion, because I know that there are people that testified today who think that the Act is perfectly fine. However, we have Mr.

Blackman here, who believes that, you know, his private property rights are being intruded on, and I think it is appropriate that we have Mr. Blackman here and someone from the Park Service, Ms. Matthews, who said in your testimony that you think it is very successful. And I think it is important to expose the feelings on this so that the members of the Committee can understand the plight of Mr. Blackman versus existing law and the problems that it is causing in the private sector.

And, Mr. Blackman, you know, I would like maybe to go in terms of this a little bit, and have some discussion in reference to—you made some pretty strong statements about National Park Service that they have retaliated against you, and I would like to know what indication do you have of this?

Mr. BLACKMAN. I have several indications. One—the—I had an architect who was working with the Virginia Department of Historic Resources. The head of that office is Kathleen Kilpatrick.

And apparently, she was ready to sign off on a draft, and this was around the time that I first contacted my Congressman, Eric Cantor. She got wind of the fact that an investigation had begun and I guess through the Park Service, and she imploded. She said basically that your client, that is I, was opening a can of worms. The Park Service was incensed by this and she would no longer be able to sign off on the proposal. Mind you, she probably did not have the right to review the plans anyway. That is neither here nor there.

Second, an acquaintance of mine, without my permission, actually called the Park Service. This woman has worked as a lobbyist in Washington. She talked to someone fairly senior in the Park Service who told her that the Park Service was going to get me. This was around the time that I was essentially cornered and contemplating litigation.

Third——

Mr. NUNES. You said someone from the Park Service said they were going to get you?

Mr. BLACKMAN. Yes.

Mr. NUNES. On the telephone?

Mr. BLACKMAN. That is what they told this woman, who's name is Diane Crawley [ph]. Now, from my perspective it is hearsay.

Mr. NUNES. Mm-hm. But obviously it is a concern to you.

Mr. BLACKMAN. Absolutely.

Third, I think if you were to read through the documents that I am providing to the Subcommittee, I think you can see from the tenor of e-mails and correspondence, some of which I obtained from a Freedom of Information Act request, that there was a retaliatory spirit. Specifically there was a letter from Marie Rust [ph] that suggests a kind of a, this motive to get me.

Mr. NUNES. OK, so Ms. Matthews, I don't know how familiar you are with Mr. Blackman's case. But, you know, this is part of the concern that happens when, I think, Government oversteps their bounds and now you have a private property owner who is very concerned about this. I don't know what you can say about this case or if you are familiar with it, but I would like to hear a response because he has made some very serious allegations and I think is being impacted.

Ms. MATTHEWS. Thank you, Mr. Chairman.

It is my understanding that this case has gone on for some time and is in litigation, and we would not be able to comment on it.

Mr. NUNES. OK. All right. Well, that makes it a little difficult to have an open and frank discussion on this matter. But—Well, my time is running out here. Mr. Blackman, could you quickly go through, in the FOIA request, what you were able to get out of there that you could expose to this Committee, what you think the top points are that came out in your request. You mentioned the e-mails. Could you talk briefly about some of the exchanges that concern you there?

Mr. BLACKMAN. Well, one of my concerns was that the Park Service was delegating and basically abrogating whatever authority they might have had to a local nonprofit group by the name of Historic Green Springs. There are a number of reasons I was concerned about this. I saw no architectural expertise in this organization, and the Park Service itself had in the 1990s expressed concerns about this organization's agenda. And so as part of the relief I was seeking, it was that the Park Service would not consult Historic Green Springs. The first response by the Park Service to the Cantor investigation was an implied promise that they would not talk to Historic Green Springs and its president. Then, in the FOIA request, I discovered e-mails in which not only did they continue consulting this woman, but they were consulting her about the response that they were drafting to me saying that they would not consult with her.

Mr. NUNES. Thank you, Mr. Blackman. My time has expired.

Ms. Christensen?

Mrs. CHRISTENSEN. Thank you, Mr. Chairman.

I might not have had any questions for Mr. Blackman, but I really need to clarify something. In your testimony, Mr. Blackman, you—I am going to read it here. "The effect of this provision is to basically run roughshod over property rights of that owner through a back-door eligibility designation."

When you purchased this property, weren't the easements already in place? Wasn't the easement already in place?

Mr. BLACKMAN. Yes. I was aware of the easement document.

Mrs. CHRISTENSEN. OK. So in actuality, the person who owned the property before had granted that easement?

Mr. BLACKMAN. No. Two owners before I purchased attempted to grant an easement. But let me mention that, while you can say I had notice of the easement document——

Mrs. CHRISTENSEN. You bought the property with the easement already there.

Mr. BLACKMAN. I don't acknowledge that the easement was effective. But I had notice of the document as well as all its frailties. I had notice of all the incoherence and ambiguities of this document. I also had notice that the prior owners had done radical things to the house without applying to the Park Service, and no objection from the Park Service. I also have to mention that there were neighbors that did things without any consequences. And I guess I did not have notice of this, that they were able to do this because they were aligned with that nonprofit organization, Historic Green Springs.

Mrs. CHRISTENSEN. Well——

Mr. BLACKMAN. But if you—I am sorry.

Mrs. CHRISTENSEN. Let me just, because the fact remains that it was in the deed under which you purchased the property.

Mr. BLACKMAN. No, it was not in the deed, Ms. Christensen. It was referred to in the deed, but it was not a part of the deed.

Mrs. CHRISTENSEN. But it was referred to, that it existed? But even beyond that, it is my understanding that the litigation in which you are involved as the defendant, that it involves the legality of the easement on this property but it doesn't have anything to do with the implementation of the National Historic Preservation Act. As a matter of fact, do any of the pleadings in your case even mention the National Historic Preservation Act?

Mr. BLACKMAN. I cannot at this moment respond to whether any of the pleadings refer to the 1966 Act, as I don't have the pleadings in front of me. But I can tell you that at an evidentiary hearing in August 2004, the Government and the Park Service referred extensively to the National Register. And frankly, one of the problems is that they seem to conflate the easement document with the National Register and the regulations created under the statute.

Mrs. CHRISTENSEN. Well, that is kind of a way around answering a question, but it is my understanding that even just looking at the case on the face of it, it really does not address the issue of the National Historic Preservation Act.

Mr. Martin, are you able to estimate generally what percentage of resources that are historically or culturally significant to Native Americans are either listed on the National Register or have been formally found eligible? And I understand the reasons why sometimes you may not want to list them. Is it a low percentage, a high percentage of significant places?

Mr. MARTIN. Ms. Christensen, there is really no way to quantify that because those statistics are not kept. I can tell you that our people were nomads. They were not a people of writing and putting things in books. It is more of an oral tradition. And those traditions were carried on in sacred places. And because they were nomads, they were very much moving. But we would suspect that there would be a very, very high percentage of sacred sites and traditional sites that our ancestors used in their practices of their religions that would be and can be affected by this change.

Mrs. CHRISTENSEN. Then they might not be listed, a good percentage might not be listed?

Mr. MARTIN. I would say the highest percentage would not be listed, because history tells us that when they are listed or even inadvertently discovered, they have been looted.

Mrs. CHRISTENSEN. Thank you, Mr. Chairman. I will come back for another round.

Mr. NUNES. Thank you, Ms. Christensen.

Mr. Radanovich.

Mr. RADANOVICH. Thank you, Mr. Chairman. And I would like to be one to congratulate you on your chairmanship of this fine Subcommittee. I enjoyed my chairmanship. And I also want to give my warm regards to my former Ranking Member, Donna Christensen. Donna, good to see you again.

Mr. Nau, I would like to address my question to you. During my time on the chairmanship of this Subcommittee—and Mr. Blackman, I am not familiar with your particular story; I apologize. I came in late today. But during the time, during last year, during my chairmanship here, we did have an example of the abuse of the historic preservation law by a group in Southern California that were using the law, I believe, to promote either a no-development or a no-growth agenda. Essentially the property owners were using these rules and regulations to prevent a developer from tearing down some apartments and rebuilding some property. In fact, I think the gentleman testified at a hearing that we had here last year.

My question to you, Mr. Nau, because I think the discussion draft, or at least the controversial parts of the discussion draft are developed to guard against the potential of abuse of something like that, especially when it comes to the area of listing potential sites. And I believe that is the motivation of the discussion draft, because I think that there is a legitimate concern. Can you address the question, because I know that you are opposed to some of the ideas in the discussion draft, being that way, can you explain to me how you think that the program can go on in a fashion that you would like to see it that would as well guard against the abuses of the program?

Mr. NAU. Thank you. Let me break your question into two parts. First, the testimony of the case of the property owner in California when I was last here. There was no question that there was a problem with that case. I will make that on the record. How did we try to deal with that in H.R. 3223, and then how was it dealt with in this discussion draft?

First, we removed the requirement that the Secretary of the Interior make a determination of eligibility for a property when a nomination is submitted over an owner's objection. As I said in my comments earlier, it makes no sense if a property owner objects. Second, it requires that the nomination process stop at the point that the owner objects and not continue. We also worked to address the issue that came from California, and that is the utilization by local jurisdictions tying their historic preservation ordinances, whatever type they might be, to this National Register process. You know, only listing on the National Register imposes no limitation on a property owner's right to modify or use Register property. It is only when that type of local ordinance is in effect that the local jurisdiction and ordinance actually kicks in. And that is what the issue was. So I think the discussion draft, picking up on H.R. 3223, deals with that issue.

The second part of your question, dealing with Section 4. I really do not believe that the elimination of potentially eligible would have properly addressed the issue raised in the California case, because it was the linkage of the local ordinance to the National Register process that kicked that in. And in this discussion draft, again, we believe that there is language that deals with that. To eliminate the potentially eligible, and where our concerns are, would eliminate thousands, tens of thousands of sites that currently are not on any list because of either resources not available to the State historic preservation officer to create that list, or, as

52

you have heard, a Native American, a Native Hawaiian, there is a dramatic reluctance to put them on any type of list.

It is fundamental to the protection to the cultural and heritage sites of this country that we have a mechanism that is flexible enough to allow sites to be located at the time that an undertaking is begun. I am a businessman, and I am from Texas, where we protect property rights as strong as any State. And it seems to me that we absolutely have to craft a flexible program that allows sites to come on, i.e., potentially eligible, while protecting the property owners and those sites and give them the opportunity to say no. And when they say no, that is it.

Thank you.

Mr. RADANOVICH. Mr. Nau, the site at the World Trade Center, would that have fallen under the potentially eligible sites portion of this or a different section in the discussion draft?

Mr. NAU. Based on Section 4 as it is written, since it is not either on the list or declared eligible, it would not have fallen under the protection of the Section 106. Neither would places like the Golden Gate Bridge, the Mission at San Juan Capistrano, the V-Site at Los Alamos, where the bomb was created. Those sites are not either declared or on. But those are critically important sites to the history of this country, and to have a system that just simply says you are either on the list or you are not important, we believe, just simply doesn't recognize the importance of thousands and thousands of sites around the United States.

Mr. RADANOVICH. All right, thank you, sir.

Mr. NAU. Thank you.

Mr. NUNES. Thank you, Mr. Radanovich.

Mr. Kildee.

Mr. KILDEE. Thank you, Mr. Chairman. And again, as I said in my opening remarks, I really appreciate the fact that you presented this as a discussion draft. I think that shows great sensitivity both to this Committee and to the public. I think it is a good procedure that others could follow.

Mr. NUNES. Thank you, Mr. Kildee.

Mr. KILDEE. Let me ask Mr. Martin, you mention that when a tribal site becomes public, it is often looted. Is that something that commonly happens once that is made public.

Mr. MARTIN. History teaches that that is a common sight. You have a segment of the population that simply every weekend in that area, that is simply what they do for their enjoyment, to go out and try to find sites.

Mr. KILDEE. What is their purpose? Is it vandalism or curiosity or a combination of both, or several motivations?

Mr. MARTIN. You have a segment of the population that is mesmerized with the Native culture. So therefore, it lends itself to a very substantial financial black market for those artifacts to be sold into for the pleasure of people to hang on their wall or keep in their safes for their private collections.

Mr. KILDEE. It seems that consulting rates are the bare minimum that are afforded tribes. Should the National Historic Preservation Act be amended to give tribes more than just consulting rates?

53

Mr. MARTIN. It is kind of ironic I am sitting here beside Mr. Blackman, because Mr. Blackman's point of view is that the Government is being too intrusive in telling him what he can do. That is not the case for American Indians. It is only consultation rights. At the end of the day, if the tribe objects, it is still the responsibility of the Federal agency. If they want to go forward, they can go forward. So we certainly, if we are going to amend the Act and if justice is to be served, let's put some teeth into it, that American Indians and Alaskan natives have the right to veto those actions in there. Certainly a minimum of consultation is the minimum. But certainly we would like to see it go forward that we would have more teeth in the law to be able to do some of the things to protect our sites.

Mr. KILDEE. This consultation takes place not only on your sovereign land, but consultation on sites that are not on your sovereign land?

Mr. MARTIN. Yes, sir, Congressman Kildee. And Congress, when it passed the amendments to the Historic Preservation Act in 1992, saw fit that wherever they existed, it gave the right of the consultation responsibility to the Federal agency to mandate that they consult with tribes irregardless of where the sites are found. And it may be that that is the reason they said it was limited to consultation in there. But certainly, that is a minimum that we feel is prevalent. This strikes at the core of our ability to be able to protect our sacred sites.

I would lean to the recent work that USET has done with the FCC in working with the Nationwide Programmatic Agreement and associated best practices that we accompanied to the programmatic agreement. We are very much in support of the FCC's efforts in that area, the creation of a National cell tower notification system wherein, if a cell tower company wants to put up a cell tower on a particular site, they can go into that data base and they will then kick out the number of tribes that that cell tower company needs to contact so that they have expressed their interest in that particular area. I can tell you, our tribes were getting in the past, when we were not—prior to the Nationwide Programmatic Agreement, getting 50 and 60 letters from cell towers on a weekly basis and typically saying, We're planning to put a cell tower here in this location. By the way, you have 10 days to respond, and if you don't respond, we believe that that is a notification to go forward.

We have worked with industry and the FCC to bring about a very time-sensitive and a responsive manner to the cell tower industry that we can consult and give them our expertise on those that they can go forward in a timely manner. To date, we believe there is over 300 Indian tribes who have submitted their areas for sensitive matter to the FCC. You know, being certainly an advocate in Indian country, if you can get 300 of the 500 tribes to submit and take on that responsibility, that is a success story.

Mr. KILDEE. Do you think we could change the language to at least strengthen the consulting rights of the tribes? Still keep it on a consultation level, maybe more than a veto level, but to strengthen the consultation rights of the tribes?

Mr. MARTIN. Certainly USET is open to that. And we are so appreciative of the Chairman putting this out as a discussion draft. And we stand ready to work with the Committee, the industry to look at how can we bring about the same protections that we enjoy, yet at the time not be perceived as obstructionist, that we can go forward in the development but yet at the time develop our future, but also to protect our past.

Mr. KILDEE. Thank you, Mr. Martin. Thank you very much.

Thank you, Mr. Chairman.

Mr. NUNES. Thank you, Mr. Kildee.

Mr. Duncan.

Mr. DUNCAN. Thank you, Mr. Chairman. This is a very important hearing, and I am sorry that other meetings kept me from getting here to hear most of the testimony.

But I can tell you that for quite some time I have been very concerned about the fact that the Federal Government now owns over 30 percent of the land in this country and State and local Governments and quasi-governmental units own another 20 percent, so you have half the land in some type of public ownership today. You can never satisfy Governments' appetite for money or land. They always want more. And we have been, especially in more recent years, very rapidly doing away with private property in this country. And if people don't realize how important private property is to our prosperity, then perhaps they should do some more reading in economics.

I am concerned about this. I didn't get my undergraduate degree before I went to law school in history, but I took so many electives in history that I could have gotten a degree in that if I had been in another college. And I am still a history buff, and I love historic preservation. I love it. But it is the few rather than the many. I have gotten in a lot of money to restore and help renovate the Tennessee Theater in Knoxville. It is a beautiful old building. But when I read things like in this Federal court decision that said a literal construction of the phrase "eligible for inclusion in the National Register" would lead almost inescapably to the conclusion that every building over 50 years old in this country is eligible for inclusion on the Register, you know, you get to a point where you almost, you become ridiculous.

For instance, it sounds so good when a politician says he wants to create a park. But we have now got so many parks in this country that we can't take care of them. And most of them are vastly under-used. And that takes property off the tax rolls, so then that increases the taxes on the property and on the people that remain on the tax rolls.

It's amazing to me that we sit around and take things from Government that we would have never taken 50 or 100 years ago. And it's amazing to me that we don't have enough people in this country that realize how important private property has been to our prosperity and our freedom. And when I read things like I do from Mr. Blackman—I didn't hear his testimony, but he said here, it says, You can do anything you wish with your house without—or it says here that the Park Service literature trumpets time and time again, and what you are being told when you are wooed to list your property on the National Register is that you can do anything you wish with your house without penalty, even demolish your house, within limits of State and local law and so forth. Alas, that is only part of the story. The National Park Service and others will use the National Register as a bludgeon against the property owner and trample his property rights if they can. To them your property, once listed, is just a resource. To them it is not a home.

And then he goes over here and says, Now, I can tell you that I am not the only person, even my community, who has encountered this morass of vague, shifting standards where most property owners end up having no choice but to give in. The Government has a huge advantage in terms of time and money when a dispute arises. The Park Service knows this. They know that they can then mess with the property owner; it does not cost them personal time or money.

And, you know, we hear this over and over again in other committees and subcommittees in addition to this one. And it's amazing to me also that people will do, without any guilt feelings whatsoever, they will do to other people what they would scream to high heaven about if it was being done to them or their property. In fact, people aren't concerned about the total taking of other people's property as long as it doesn't touch them. They don't realize how hurtful it is personally. And I am not up here saying these things because me or anybody in my family has had this happen. But I sure have seen it happen to a lot of other people.

And we have a real problem here when we hear Government agents come here and tell us that there are no restrictions or limitations, and then we hear from property owners all over the country and in our districts that these Government bureaucrats want to come in and, unless the people bow down to them and kiss their rear ends, then they trample all over them. And we hear things like "out to get" them. And, you know, this is supposed to be a Governance of, by, and for the people; it is not supposed to be a Government of, by, and for the bureaucrats. Or it is not supposed to be a Government where, if somebody thinks that your property has some historic value, they can come in and just say, well, you can't do what to do with your property. You can't even fix it up. It's ridiculous.

Thank you, Mr. Chairman.

Mr. NUNES. Thank you, Mr. Duncan.

Mr. Altschul, you provide an example in your testimony how the Historic Preservation Act can create serious threats to public safety. In your opinion, how do we ensure that the Historic Preservation Act, particularly the Section 106 process, does not hamper our Nation's first responders?

Mr. ALTSCHUL. Well, obviously the public safety wireless users rely on the same laws of physics as the commercial users. So you can't have radio communications without towers and structures. What we all need is certainty and finality to the review process. As I mentioned in my testimony, in nearly every case, to erect such a structure we go through an extensive local zoning and review process. Then there is this separate Section 106 process. If Section 106 was restored to the original intent of Congress, where items are listed or listed as being eligible by the keeper, it would begin to provide that kind of certainty that we require.

Mr. NUNES. So what suggestions do you have? I mean, you have seen the draft discussion on 106. So would your organization tend to support the changes that have been in 106, or do they have other alternatives that would be helpful?

Mr. ALTSCHUL. No, we certainly do support the changes proposed in Section 4 of the discussion draft. We also acknowledge and respect the unique situation and challenge of protection, preserving sites of religious and cultural importance to tribes. We respect their sovereignty and their right to seek Government-to-Government consultation anytime during the process. I think that is something that we would need to pursue as part of the discussion draft.

Mr. NUNES. Thank you.

Could you discuss the Western Maryland case?

Mr. ALTSCHUL. Yes. There is a very small town—calling it a "town" may dignify it—called Lambs Knoll, Maryland, in Western Maryland. There was a 3-year delay while the Section 106 process was pending and ultimately had to be brought to the attention of the Governor of Maryland, brought it to the FCC for resolution. It was a tower site that was going to be shared by both public safety and commercial wireless users. And public safety communications were being degraded to the point that the MedEvac helicopter crews were unable to the communicate on their rescue missions with the public safety first responders. Despite the urgency and the clear public need, the Section 106 process dragged on and on. As I said, it required the intervention of the Governor of Maryland and the expedited review by the FCC that found that there was no 106 issue that merited delaying the approval of the site.

Mr. NUNES. Thank you, Mr. Altschul. I just had one other question that I think is kind of interesting for discussion. If one of your towers was 50 years old, would it be your understanding that they would be potentially eligible under the current definition of the act?

Mr. ALTSCHUL. Well, it is not a hypothetical question. We actually do have some towers that are 50 years old. Western Union Telegraph erected them. And just like the expression, one person's wildflower is another person's weeds, there is a person who wishes to preserve some of these towers—aren't being used and could be in disrepair and should be brought down—and in fact challenge plans to tear down one of these old towers. That also made its way to the FCC after a protracted review process, and the FCC did the right thing and approved the demolition of the tower.

Mr. NUNES. That is very interesting. Thank you.

Ms. Christensen is recognized.

Mrs. CHRISTENSEN. Thank you, Mr. Chair.

A real quick question to Mr. Martin. Mr. Martin, you have said at least twice that you are willing to work with the Committee to address some of the issues raised in the discussion draft. But is it your position that there are things that need to be changed in the act? I mean, we had introduced reauthorization last year without any changes. Would you support that?

Mr. MARTIN. Certainly. We would review those and we would comment on those to make sure if it is an improvement and to make certain in clarity. We would like to bring about clarity, bring about consistency that certain sets of facts that appear across the United States ought to render the same decisions.

Mrs. CHRISTENSEN. But you wouldn't weaken the authority of the Act to preserve any of the cultural and historical treasures of the country?

Mr. MARTIN. No, ma'am. And what we have to realize is those four little words is the core, is the platform to which we utilize the ability to be able to be consulted—and only consulted if we are going to change the Act right now. It is not a Federal undertaking to put up a cell tower. It is a Federal undertaking if you are going to put an antenna on that cell wire, which needs the Federal licensing. Now, we can make a great improvement to that, that if the construction of a cell tower for the purpose of hanging an antenna on it becomes a Federal action, then we will go much further than what exists right now in there.

But we are very much appreciative of the cell tower industries— like Sprint, who is working with tribes to expeditiously review the sites and working with their subcontractors—say don't build this tower if you are going to come back later and tell us you haven't followed the 106 process. We are encouraged by CTIA, who is saying they respect tribal sovereignty in our ability to consult on a Government-to-Government basis.

So I believe there is room to study this matter to see what is needed, why it is needed, as we protect our sacred sites also.

Mrs. CHRISTENSEN. Thank you.

Mr. Altschul, please give our regards to Mr. Largent. We are sorry to hear that he is not well.

Mr. ALTSCHUL. Thank you.

Mrs. CHRISTENSEN. In your testimony, you provide examples of cases in which a State historic preservation officer found a site under consideration for a new cell tower was inappropriate because it might impact historic resources, but where the SHPO's concerns were later determined to be unfounded. I am sure that that is not a completely exhaustive list, that there are cases—you would have to admit that there are many cases where the findings were upheld.

Mr. ALTSCHUL. Yes.

Mrs. CHRISTENSEN. So I am trying to just clarify your position. Is it your position that we should amend the Act to make it more difficult for the SHPOs to delay placement of cell towers in sensitive areas even though there are so many instances where the SHPO had that authority and saved historic resources from harm. Is it your position that we should make it more difficult?

Mr. ALTSCHUL. Absolutely not. What we are here today to urge this Subcommittee to do is to restore some certainty and finality to the process. We recognize our obligation, not just under the law but as citizens of the communities that we serve and intend to serve for many, many years, to respect these historic and cultural resources. But what we object to is the inability during the construction and siting of towers to have any certainty as to what sites are going to be razed, sites that have not been brought to the keeper and have not been designated as being eligible for——

Mrs. CHRISTENSEN. But I am sure you can appreciate that not everything that has cultural and historical value in the country is on the list and that there is value in, for example, the Native

American sites that may be 50,000 years old but are not listed being protected.

Mr. ALTSCHUL. Well, CTIA does recognize particularly the tribal sites, and we have pledged today and we have pledged before today to work with Mr. Martin and the tribes on their unique needs. But with respect to the tens of millions of potentially eligible sites, anything over 50 years old, I think we all learn as children and then teach our children that if everything is deemed special, nothing is special. And the original intent of Congress in passing this Act, I believe, was to really designate those properties which deserve the recognition and protection of this Act.

Mrs. CHRISTENSEN. But I think that what it requires is that you look before you destroy. Not that everything is sacred, but that you look at and determine first whether there are some historical and cultural sites that ought to be preserved before you go ahead.

I appreciate, you know, your willingness to work with the tribes, the association's willingness to work with the tribes, but it just seems—I mean, when you are gone and somebody else is there, or Mr. Largent is gone and someone else is there, it seems that the protection of the law, you know, ensures that that process continues.

Mr. ALTSCHUL. Well, we are committed. I obviously speak for all of us here today. The other reality is that tribal lands are some of the least well-served in terms of telecommunications services in our country. And there is a mutual interest, I believe, to develop good relations that are respectful of the tribal lands and allow the industry to deliver these 21st century services, to provide the services that the tribes desire and want. I think that is a fact that, more important than any law, is going to ensure we make progress in this area.

Mr. MARTIN. Ms. Christensen, I would like to comment on that. He is correct. The American Indian, Alaska native areas are some of the ill-served, certainly, by the cell tower industry at this time, and they have made a commitment.

A point in example: My tribe is in South Alabama. Not too long ago, we had an uninvited guest come into that area in the form of Andrew. For the first 48 hours after Andrew came into there, there was only, in a sense, two cell phones that worked. And that was the communication link for my tribe of 2,200 people.

So Native America is certainly receptive to the need and the progress of cell tower, but we should do it as we keep in balance our past also with that development of the future.

Mrs. CHRISTENSEN. And we are very sensitive to that. I know I am running out of time, but one question I would have had for Mr. Nau or anyone is to cite for us if there is any area that evidences Section 106 is not functioning as it should function so that the services can be provided and the sites protected and everybody wins.

Mr. NUNES. Thank you, Ms. Christensen.

Mr. Kildee.

Mr. KILDEE. One final question for myself. Ms. Wadhams, how significant will the effect of Section 4 of the discussion draft have on Indian tribes?

59

Ms. WADHAMS. As I mentioned in my testimony and as you heard from Mr. Martin earlier, it would be extremely significant, in our opinion. The effect would be extremely significant because of the lack of listings of traditional cultural properties and archeological sites and the difficulty of even knowing in some cases where these sites are.

Mr. KILDEE. So for that reason, they would be more vulnerable to negative effects?

Ms. WADHAMS. They would be arguably more vulnerable, and we are very concerned and, for that reason alone, think this change to Section 4 would be very problematic. It would also impact buildings, however. I think there was an issue before of, you know, how can we improve this process. I think one way to improve this process would be to give more funds to State historic preservation offices and the THPOs, the tribes, to do the survey work that is necessary. Having been a former State historic preservation officer, I know that we work from a triage approach to our Federal responsibilities. We have a lot of responsibilities under the National Historic Preservation Act. Survey is one of them. Section 106, providing technical assistance, and reviewing projects for historic tax credits are some of the things we do. And if you have a Section 106 review here and you have doing survey work here, the Section 106 is always going to take precedence just because of the pressing need to do those in an expeditious manner.

So the survey work often doesn't get done because—or it happens every day. It is happening in SHPO offices every day. But it is going to get triaged out. And the funding has not been adequate to the SHPOs and the THPOs to do this work. It has actually decreased over the years. So it is the first thing that doesn't happen. And a way to improve this to some degree—it wouldn't get rid of all the concerns that you have heard about, but we also believe those concerns are fairly unusual. If there were more funding to do the survey work, it would help with these issues, and actually list properties on the National Register.

So I think there are ways to approach this that could help without actually changing the National Historic Preservation Act.

Mr. KILDEE. Thank you very much.

And again, Mr. Chairman, thank you for the very sensitive process you have used in developing this bill. Thank you.

Mr. NUNES. Thank you, Mr. Kildee.

Ms. Wadhams, from 1974 to 1976, "eligible for inclusion" was to find in the ACHP rules as any district site, et cetera, which the Secretary determines is likely to meet the National Register criteria. Then in 1979, without authorization from Congress, ACHP changed the definition to "property eligible for inclusion" to mean any property that meets the National Register criteria.

Would you not agree that these and other ACHP rules eliminated the National Register from relevance and instead created a reliance on consensus determinations of eligibility?

Ms. WADHAMS. To some degree, yes. And remember, this is— Section 106 mandates a process. It doesn't mandate an outcome. And it also requires people to work in good faith together to try to get to some outcomes. So the process is extremely critical and

60

important in resolving this issue. I don't know if this answers your question. Maybe you would like to expand a little bit.

Mr. NUNES. Well, I just—you know, we have a letter here that was, I think, submitted from the record from this coalition of 9/11 families. And someone brought up the example that, oh, this maybe would not be eligible under the Historic Preservation Act. But the changes that are in the discussion draft that would say essentially, that would just define it as being or determined by the Secretary to be eligible for inclusion. It think it is a little—you know, I don't like when people use these examples, because I don't believe that any Secretary would not deem the World Trade Center as not being eligible.

Ms. WADHAMS. I think the World Trade Center, as I said, is a dramatic and compelling example and is not typical. But it does point out the fact that if you just look at listed properties, properties listed on the National Register, there are properties from the World Trade Center to an archeological site, perhaps the oldest farming site in the State of Vermont, which was discovered through the 106 process. For example. We never knew when they started actually doing agriculture in the State, and through a highway project and the need to do 106, we found the site that proved that this is when agriculture started in the State.

So there is a—with just the eligibility language, as is proposed in this, there is no process. The process would be excluded. And that is the point I was trying to make with the World Trade Center site, is the process was in place for the—specifically the families of the victims, and the public, to be able to say, OK, is this a historic site? It is not listed. Nobody had even thought about it. But in fact it is a critical site to our Nation's history. So that process was there and in place and could be used to make that determination fairly quickly and involve the people who wanted to have a say in what might happen to the site.

If you take out the "or eligible for inclusion in the National Register," the process isn't there. It is not that it might not have happened in some way, shape, or form down the road, but it was there and we could use it to engage the public.

Mr. NUNES. Well, I think that is part of the problem with private property owners, is that sometimes this is being used by cities and other agencies to hang up development, you know, to stop development or to stop putting up cell phone towers. And, you know, one problem I think we have here is that in 1979, when this was changed, you know, it was changed without review from this Committee. And not that that was a major problem; those things do happen. But, you know, we have gone along for decades now, and now, unfortunately I think—Ms. Matthews, in your testimony you said that less than 1 percent of what is deemed eligible actually becomes eligible. I think—"There are 617,000 Federal projects that went through Section 106 in a 5-year period. Only 1.5 percent resulted in nominations to the Register." And so, you know, that just leads me to believe why would so many sites be put up for inclusion to this and so few being actually included?

Ms. MATTHEWS. Well, exactly the intent of the law itself, is in a Federal undertaking in the 1970s under President Nixon, there was an Executive Order that expanded the determinations of eligibility to go into Federal agencies taking into consideration their own Federal agency's undertaking as it impacted other Federal agencies. And just as Emily cited, in highway constructions in Florida, we have discovered things we didn't know before. And——

Mr. NUNES. I understand that. But wouldn't the Secretary under this change in the law still have the ability to, if something was discovered when you are building a freeway or a road, wouldn't they have the ability to add it to the historic preservation list?

Ms. MATTHEWS. Yes, but exactly as Emily said, the process starts clicking away when the project begins. There is a great cooperation among the Federal entities and the State, as the State historical preservation office is a Federal entity, to look at prior-to documentation, which can take a long time, often is not done, on properties where it might never be done because there isn't a comprehensive survey in any State except Rhode Island completed. And so it is an ongoing process, where a country in which there are so many resources that we haven't surveyed for significance, determined to be eligible or not eligible, and taking these into consideration in Federal undertakings is a very critical process.

And it was undertaken because there was such a loss to communities. We know today heritage tourism is a huge economic engine. We did a study in Florida on the economic impacts of heritage tourism that Mr. Nau and Secretary of the Interior Gale Norton have used in demonstrations that heritage tourism is economically beneficial. And we were able to demonstrate that $4.2 billion annually was returned to the State of Florida through economic impacts of heritage tourism. And much of that arises out of that process.

Mr. NUNES. I don't disagree with that, and I am not discounting that. I am just—you know, my question is that there seems to be such a large number of these projects that are being nominated and then so very few are actually being put onto the list. Which, you know, kind of leads—and it would be interesting, I think—I don't have the numbers to go back, you know, 20 years ago, how many that were nominated actually were included. And I think the point that some of these private property owners are making or the telecom industry is making is that sometimes this is being used as a legal tactic to stop development or stop someone from fixing their house, whatever it may be.

You know, how many more sites or historic sites are out there that have not been put on the list? I guess we don't know. There is probably an infinite number. But I mean, if you look throughout the United States, there is a lot of them now. And, you know, where is this going to stop and why are so many being nominated? I mean, there has got to be a problem here with this process. I think to just say we don't need any changes is, you know, a little bit kind of just protecting maybe your own turf and not being willing to work with the private property owners.

Ms. MATTHEWS. I have come from several decades of work as a historical consultant on projects that were either for private property owners or 106 projects for cultural resource management firms. And I have seen over the years in my career a huge benefit of just the heritage tourism aspect, the understanding of our land. We are uniquely a country that recognizes local significance through the National Historic Preservation Act, where at one time we only recognized national historic landmarks, things of national importance. We are now very concerned about we as a Nation—we as private and public—very concerned about neighborhoods, your grandmother's house if it qualifies, and the diversity of our heritage assets. And that is an ongoing study. Just as history is never static, neither are the things that are included. Decades ago, tribal, Native American, Native Hawaiian, Native Alaskans were not taken into consideration under the law; currently they have an equal role on the Native American Grave Protection and Repatriation Act review committee, through that Act, which is 1990s. We as a Nation, as a democracy evolve in how we look at ourselves.

And I think we could get you some better statistics on your specific question, on the percentage. I would be happy to do so, Mr. Chairman.

Mr. NUNES. Thank you. I do want to read something here, Ms. Matthews, that was submitted for the record. And forgive me, because I have not read this before, so I am going to have to look at it here.

Here it says—this is an example. There was a woman on the Register in September 1996. The banks declined to give them a mortgage for their alterations to make the changes to the 1830s house into a bed & breakfast on the grounds that the building was on the National Historic Register. Finally, they approached their congressman for help. The only solution which was in his hands, Mr. Roach told me, was to have the house deleted from the National Historic Register. The congressman used his influence to have the historic registration for the house finally removed and the bank gave the mortgage to the family.

So I assume that this is an ongoing problem with the Act that—can you comment on that?

Ms. MATTHEWS. I can. I will be happy to get back with you on information related specifically to that.

Mr. NUNES. OK. Well, we will submit this in writing to you after this hearing.

Ms. MATTHEWS. Thank you, Mr. Chairman.

Mr. NUNES. The largest criticism this Committee has had over this discussion draft has been the Section 106. Many have proposed that this will shatter the consensus determinations under the 106 process. This is what, you know, we are hearing from the preservation community.

I guess, you know, what I am looking at is, you know, I fail to see the problem by the proposed language that clearly does not prohibit nor impede SHPO survey work to identify and nominate eligible properties to the Register or make recommendations of eligibility to the secretaries required under the Act—which I have commented on already. But I think there is a misunderstanding between, at least from my point of view and statements that have been made in regard to that this small change to Section 106 would cause all these disastrous things from happening. Ms. Matthews, can you comment more on this?

Ms. MATTHEWS. I think as part of our statement as well, 70 percent of the properties that are taken into consideration in Federal activities were not specifically listed or determined eligible. It is a big percentage. And we also have, while we are commenting on that—let me go back to this common theme of the uniqueness of our National Historic Preservation Act, your National Historic Preservation Act—is that we have in the local significance—we have local, State, and Federal significance as levels of significance under the Act—and that we have almost 70 percent as well of the properties listed on the National Register, 1.4 million, within 79,000 listings total to date, and that is because, as you know, 79,000 listings include many contributing resources within neighborhoods, which are very important in communities.

And I think that speaks for itself. The potentially eligible often occurs and it is not the actual survey or the documentation. I mean, we have done in the private sector nominations, documentations on significance that, I think our estimate in Florida is it is $2,500 a year or so to do documentation on a National Register. A Federal highway project coming in needs to do something a lot quicker than that. And in Florida, we set a 30-day turnaround time, which is required by law, under all of our compliance for review of 106 considerations. Governor Bush had us expedite that. Secretary of State Harris had us expedite that. And we moved those things very fast.

Mr. NUNES. Thank you, Ms. Matthews.

Mr. ALTSCHUL. Can I comment on your question as well?

Mr. NUNES. Yes, Mr. Altschul, please.

Mr. ALTSCHUL. Your question was about what happens to these sites of significance, should Section 106 be restored to what I read as the original congressional intent.

First and foremost, the wireless industry, I can speak with great confidence, has an independent obligation to consult with the tribes separate from the 106 process.

Second, we have heard today Section 106 does create a process and it creates that process whether the end result is a listing that is brought to the keeper of the Secretary of the Interior for determination as being eligible or being put on the list, or what this process has become, which has become an uncertain, never-ending morass for industries like the wireless industry.

Finally, we heard about the Executive Order and the original intent of the Act in 1966. At that time, it was well understood that Congress and President Nixon were talking about Federal undertakings—road constructions, the Big Dig in Boston that has been going on for, you know, a lifetime——

Mr. NUNES. Yes, we know about that here. I would like to have about 10 percent of that money for my district.

Mr. ALTSCHUL. Right. It is going on here in Springfield. And so these are clear Federal undertakings, they have Federal funding, a beginning, a start, a review process. We have heard how wireless sites are different. There is this irony that you can build a tower for tourism or sightseeing and not be subject to this Act, but if you want to hang an antenna upon it, suddenly you are deemed subject to the Section 106 process.

So that is the kind of mission creep which has really gone beyond the original intent of Congress, and something that this Committee should address.

Mr. NUNES. Thank you, Mr. Altschul.

Mr. NAU. Mr. Chairman?

Mr. NUNES. Yes, Mr. Nau, I actually have a question for you. But go ahead and respond.

Mr. NAU. You are the chair.

Mr. NUNES. No, you are recognized to respond.

Mr. NAU. I think it is important that I do respond to the last series of comments being made, because it leaves the impression that this 106 process is old, inflexible, and restrictive, particularly restrictive on new industries. I would like to point out to the chair that in 2001, the ACHP actually crafted new regulations that specifically recognized the need to begin to create a way for the 106 process and the National Historic Preservation Act to react to the changing times. You are correct. It isn't 50 years ago, it isn't 100 years ago, and things are moving a lot faster.

What tools were created? We have programmatic agreements, alternate procedures, program comments, and exemptions. Since my chairmanship, we have used alternate procedures to help the Army with their management of their historic properties. Program comments, particularly to deal with the—housing and the DOD. Exempting programs. The very first issue I faced was the historic gas pipelines. Didn't seem to me to be somewhat logical to say that something underground is going to have a dramatic impact on preservation and heritage tourism. The fact of the matter is that it did have a dramatic effect on winning the Second World War. The issue was the story, not the pipeline itself. And we used that exemption. And the interstate highway system, same thing. If you have ever been in West Texas, there is nothing really redeeming about I-10 across the Chihuahuan Desert.

[Laughter.]

Mr. NAU. But there are parts that are worth saving, and therefore the system has flexibility.

The last one I would like to talk about is the agreement with the FCC on cell towers, because the problems that the gentleman has identified actually did exist. Now, if we had just sat down and didn't pay any attention to the issues, I would suggest that you have the obligation, not just the right, to start asking us questions. But what did we do to try to address the issue? We sat down with the FCC and the cell tower industry—I personally did it, because I carry a lot of cell phones, so I want to make sure I can talk to people. And we crafted, through these procedures and the programmatic agreements, and addressed the issue that the gentleman identified, and that is certainty. He was talking about certainty of numbers of assets. I would suggest it wasn't just number, it is location. And certainty of time, from a businessman's standpoint, is where the cost is.

Through that agreement, we crafted the first-ever requiring SHPOs to answer the questions within 30 days. It isn't unlimited, as the implication might be; it is definitive to 30 days because that makes sense. There the SHPO has to identify it and craft that for-certain list that I think ultimately will be the end result of any one of these types of projects. So to say that there isn't the management flexibility in the 106 process right now, I think, is to not understand the tools that we do have.

One final comment. I also am chairman of the office in Texas for the SHPO. And you raised a very good question: Why, if we have

all of these undertakings, has the list not expanded? It is purely
an issue of resources. It takes money and time and people to process the National Register application. And I will tell you, in Texas
we simply don't have the resources to do it. This isn't a request for
funding. I may be the only one up here that is not asking for
money. But it is critical to recognize the potentially eligible allows
people with vested interest, be it business, the SHPO, tribes, and
local residents, to identify those resources, figure out how to deal
with them in that undertaking. And whether or not they are submitted for eligibility, the process works.

And I would reiterate what some of the other witnesses here
have said. If you change the process, you do dramatic harm to all
of those resources that are out there, Mr. Chairman, that we don't
have on a list. And I agree with you, they are not on a list. But
they are pretty easy to identify once you start the process.

Thank you very much.

Mr. NUNES. Well, Mr. Nau, thank you. I wanted to—you actually
answered the question I was going to ask. I know that your advisory council has come up with some remedies to address these concerns, so I was going to ask you that question. And thank you for
answering it.

I do, however, want to go back a little bit to the change in 1979
which was supposed to go through this Committee and it wasn't.
And I think it is important that everyone who is interested in historic preservation look at ways that we can alter 106 to get a clear
authorization from the Congress on how this is going to—on how
we are going to proceed from here. And that doesn't mean that this
discussion draft is ultimately the bill that we are going to intro-
duce, but I do think it is important that all of you work with the
Committee staff to try to come up with some language that clarifies
some of the changes that have been made without authorization of
this Committee.

Mr. NAU. Well, thank goodness that was some other chairman
that did that in 1979. We look forward to working, as we have
been, with the staff. There is nothing that is perfect, and we recognize that by saying that we do need to change some of the elements
that have the impact on property rights. We recognize that. But
the law of unintended consequences may be at the real heart of our
concern with the Section 4.

So thank you very much.

Mr. NUNES. Thank you, Mr. Nau. And I want to thank—I do
have to get to the Capitol, but I want to thank all of you for your
testimony today. If you have additional testimony, please send it to
the Committee in writing.

This hearing is adjourned.

[Whereupon, at 11:53 a.m., the Subcommittee was adjourned.]

NOTE: The following information submitted for the record has
been retained in the Committee's official files.

- Andrews-Maltais, Cheryl, Tribal Historic Preservation Officer,
  Wampanoag Tribe of Gayhead Aquinnah, Statement submitted
  for the record
- Arthur, George, Chairman, Resources Committee of The
  Navajo Nation Council, Statement submitted for the record

- Barbry, Earl, Tribal Historic Preservation Officer, Tunica-Biloxi Tribe of Louisiana, Statement submitted for the record
- Bense, Judith, President, Society for Historical Archaeology, Group Letter, Individual Letter, and Statement submitted for the record
- Boyd, Douglas, Vice President, Prewitt and Associates, Inc., Cultural Resources Services, Group Letter and Statement submitted for the record
- Brien, Cora, James Madison University, Statement submitted for the record
- Burns, Laura, Citizen, Statement submitted for the record
- Burrow, Ian, President, American Cultural Resources Association, Group Letter, Individual Letter, and Statement submitted for the record
- Campbell, Bradley, Commissioner, State of New Jersey Department of Environmental Protection, Statement submitted for the record
- Cast, Robert, Tribal Historic Preservation Officer, Caddo Nation of Oklahoma, Statement submitted for the record
- Concho, Raymond, Governor, Pueblo of Acoma, Written Statement for the record
- Daingkau, George, Chairman, United Tribes of Colorado, Statement submitted for the record
- Faucheux, Ron, Vice President for Government Affairs, American Institute of Architects, Group Letter and Statement submitted for the record
- Fesler, Garrett, Senior Archaeologist, James River Institute for Archaeology, Inc., Group Letter and Statement submitted for the record
- Fields, Ross, President, Prewitt and Associates, Inc., Cultural Resources Services, Group Letter and Statement submitted for the record
- Francis, Melvin, Chief/Sakom, Pleasant Point Reservation, Statement submitted for the record
- Gardner, Karen, Vice President, Prewitt and Associates, Inc., Cultural Resources Services, Group Letter and Statement submitted for the record
- Garrett, Cathy, Principal, PGA Design Landscape Architects, Statement submitted for the record
- Gilreath, Amy, President, Society for California Archaeologists, Statement submitted for the record
- Goldstein, Nick, Staff Attorney, American Road and Transportation Builders Association, Statement submitted for the record
- Goodwin, Christopher, President and CEO, R. Christopher Goodwin and Associates, Inc., Group Letter and Statement submitted for the record
- Halsey, John, State Archaeologist, Michigan Historical Center, Statement submitted for the record
- Hamrick, James, Assistant Director of Heritage Conservation, Deputy State Historic Preservation Office, State of Oregon, Statement submitted for the record
- Johnson, Anthony, Chairman, Nez Perce Tribal Executive Committee, Statement submitted for the record

- Johnson, Barbara, President, San Antonio Conservation Society, Statement submitted for the record
- Johnson, Jacqueline, Executive Director, National Congress of American Indians, Statement submitted for the record
- Kraus, Bambi, President, National Association of Tribal Historic Preservation Officers, Group Letter, Individual Letter, and Statement submitted for the record
- Kulongosky, Theodore, Governor, State of Oregon, Statement submitted for the record
- Laird, Matthew, Senior Researcher, James River Institute for Archaeology, Inc., Group Letter and Statement submitted for the record
- LeBlanc, Alton, Chairman, Chitimacha Tribe of Louisiana, Statement submitted for the record
- Lewis, George, President, Ho-Chunk Nation, State of Oregon, Statement submitted for the record
- Linderner, Christopher, President, New York Archaeological Council, Group Letter and Statement submitted for the record
- Lintz, Christopher, Senior Principal Investigator, Cultural Resources Division, Geo-Marine, Inc., Statement submitted for the record
- Luccketti, Nicholas, Principal Archaeologist, James River Institute for Archaeology, Inc., Group Letter and Statement submitted for the record
- Luckerman, Douglas, Attorney at Law, Law Office of Douglas J. Luckerman, Statement submitted for the record
- MacIntosh, Heather, President, Preservation Action, Group Letter, Individual Letter, and Statement submitted for the record
- McNerney, Michael, President and Staff, American Resources Group, Statement submitted for the record
- Miller, Kevin, President, Council of Texas Archeologists, Statement submitted for the record
- Moe, Richard, President, National Trust for Historic Preservation, Group Letter and Statement submitted for the record
- Motsinger, Tom. Vice President, SWCA Environmental Consultants, Group Letter and Statement submitted for the record
- Nenema, Glen, Chairman, Kalispel Tribe of Indians, Statement submitted for the record
- Niquette, Charles, President, Cultural Resource Analysts, Inc., Statement submitted for the record
- Pakoota, Joseph, Chair, Colville Business Council, Statement submitted for the record
- Patterson, Brian, Bear Clan Representative, Oneida Indian Nation, Statement submitted for the record
- Polk, Ann, Senior Archaeologist/Owner, Sagebrush Consultants, LLC, Statement submitted for the record
- Polk, Michael, Principal/Owner, Sagebrush Consultants, LLC., Statement submitted for the record
- Quin, Richard, Citizen, Statement submitted for the record
- Rotenstein, David, Citizen, Statement submitted for the record

- Ryan, Edward, Director, Wireless Communications, State of Maryland, Department of Budget and Management, Office of Information Technology, Statement submitted for the record
- Sansom, Robert, Private Property Owner in Louisa and Greene Counties, Letter submitted for the record
- Schroeder, Eric, Citizen, Statement submitted for the record
- Shamu, Nancy, Executive Director, National Conference of State Historic Preservation Officers, Group Letter and Statement submitted for the record
- Shije, Amadeo, Chairman, All Indian Pueblo Council Office of the Chairman, Statement submitted for the record
- Tyrer, Carol. Operations Manager Curator, James River Institute for Archaeology, Inc., Group Letter and Statement submitted for the record
- Van West, Carla, Senior Principal Investigator and Research Director, Statistical Research, Inc., Statement submitted for the record
- Vaughn, Charles, Tribal Chairman, Haulapai Nation Office of the Chairman, Statement submitted for the record
- Versaggi, Nina, Chair, Standards Committee, New York Archaeological Council, Group Letter and Statement submitted for the record
- Vogt, Jay, President, South Dakota State Historic Preservation Officer, National Conference of State Historic Preservation Officers, Statement submitted for the record
- Wade, Bill, Chair, The Coalition of National Park Service Retirees Executive Council, Statement submitted for the record
- Wade, Faye, President, Archeological Society of Virginia, Statement submitted for the record
- Waldbaum, Jane, President, Archaeological Institute of America, Statement submitted for the record
- Widdiss, Donald, Chairman, Wampanoag Tribe of Gayhead Aquinnah, Statement submitted for the record
- Wilson, Dr. Sherrill, Director, Office of Public Education & Interpretation, New York African Burial Ground Project, Statement submitted for the record.

○

CPSIA information can be obtained
at www.ICGtesting.com
Printed in the USA
LVHW101602220621
690864LV00005B/323

9 781240 503186